A MONTH
OF SUNDAES

A MONTH OF SUNDAES

by Michael Turback

R E D R O C K P R E S S
New York

A MONTH OF SUNDAES
by Michael Turback

Copyright © 2002 Michael Turback

ISBN: 0-9669573-8-5
LOC: 2001095471

Published by Red Rock Press
New York, New York
U.S.A.

www.RedRockPress.com

Cover photograph: Getty Images © 2002

Back cover art: Large detail of painting by Freeman Elliot which appeared on March 1956 cover of *Calling All Girls*, published by Parents Magazine, by permission of Jeff Luther, PC design.

Thank you to the following:

Barbara Leveroni, Franchise Associates, Inc., South Weymouth, Massachusetts, for granting use of excerpts from Howard Johnson's Fountain Service Manual and related materials.

Alan Rosen, Junior's of Brooklyn, for allowing use of the Mountain High Sundae recipe, which also is in *Welcome to Junior's* by Marvin and Walter Rosen, published in 1999 by William Morrow and Company.

"A Banana Split for My Baby" by Louis Prima and Stan Irwin. Copyright © 1956. Renewed and assigned 1984 to LGL Music administered by Larry Spier, Inc., New York, N.Y. Reprinted with permission.

Richard Stewart, President of the Gumbo Shop, New Orleans, Louisiana, for allowing use of the Praline Sundae recipe, which also is in his cookbook, *Gumbo Shop*, published by the restaurant in 1999.

Connie Berman of Media, Pennsylvania, for allowing use of the Hot Fudge Bagel Supreme recipe, which is also in *Bagelmania* by Connie Berman and Suzanne Munshower, published in 1987 by HP Books.

PRINTED IN THE UNITED STATES OF AMERICA

Acknowledgements

This entire work is really an acknowledgement because it is meant to express my love for Ithaca, New York, the place where I have spent my entire adult life, the place where I have made my truest friendships.

A Month of Sundaes could not have been written anywhere else, and for this reason I wish to acknowledge a deep debt of gratitude to the resources and staff of the Tompkins County Library, to Cornell University and the Hotel School Library, and to the Dewitt Historical Society. It would be impossible for me to list all the people who have put up with all my questions, and those who have given me the benefit of their wisdom and recollections, but I must especially thank Jeffrey Turback, Craig Goldwyn, Joe Calderone, Tim Schumacher, Blaine Hopkins, Sylvia Baumgarten, Sylvia Carter, Barbara Lang, Morgan Barth, Thelma Nopoulos, Bonnie Warren, David Jackson, Rose Sgarlato, Kim Goeller-Johnson, Scott Brady and Jamie Farr.

I am grateful to my editor, Ilene Barth, for her support and guidance, and to agent Madeleine Morel for introducing us. I thank my research assistants, Jane Suh, Patrick Ro, Kate Hawley, and Joshua Romalis, who helped me fit the pieces of the puzzle into place.

Finally, a special thanks to my wife, Juliet—a Strawberry Sundae of a woman.

-Michael Turback

PREFACE

So much about eating a Sundae is instinctively about happy memories. If I close my eyes, I can recall the excitement as our family Studebaker pulled up to the Carvel Ice Cream drive-in on the way home from a day at the Jersey Shore. I remember the astonishing mound of smooth vanilla ice cream blanketed by warm, gooey chocolate sauce topped by billows of whipped cream and a bright red cherry. My dear mother always said that it wasn't summer until you ate your first banana split. There is so much joy connected to those Sundae summers of my youth that to me the Sundae has always been more than just another dessert.

And now, having thought about and enjoyed Sundaes these many years, I've concluded that the Sundae really is the great American treat, symbolic of our abundance and appetite, our ingenuity, our never-lost youth.

After I arrived in Ithaca, New York, to attend Cornell at the age of seventeen, I discovered that Ithaca was where the Ice Cream Sundae had been invented. But this news was not presented with a sense of pride. Rather, I had a Hungarian professor whose Restaurant Management lectures berated the American sins against European culinary tradition. He explained that only in America would someone think of inflicting hot fudge sauce upon ice cream. Eager as I was to be a food sophisticate— and it is something I believe I've achieved—I recognized even then that my teacher's snobbery lacked understanding of true taste delight.

During my nearly thirty-year career as a restaurateur in Ithaca, I collected recipes, sketches, anecdotes and minutiae about Sundae-making. I have devoted an embarrassing amount of time to eating and thinking about eating ice cream. But it was not until I started mulling over this material that I recognized all the attributes of the Sundae that make it so original, enduring and authentically American.

The Sundae is, or can be, everything good at once—and almost always the eater gets to choose each last ingredient. What is more democratic than that? Moreover, the Sundae is elaborate-looking but wonderfully easy to prepare. It also satisfies our penchant for the fancy and plain, the traditional and the original, at the same time.

It is my conclusion that the Sundae is an art form—uncommonly inventive, exceptionally appealing and (for the most part) democratically priced. To write about the Sundae, I have learned, is to consider several aspects of American history. Insofar as Sundaes are us, then the changes in their ingredients and presentation also tell us something about the country's permutations and aspirations as the decades go by.

In the 21st century, the Sundae still seems to me a sublime creation. In one sense, as fast foods have gotten even faster, the Sundae has folded inward, its sauce and other nuggets pre-streaked and spiked into the ice cream, which has been stuffed into a cone and then dipped into or sprinkled with yet more toppings. But there are plenty of places, from longstanding drugstore soda fountains to newly-popular "classic" diners to fine restaurants, that still offer glass-dished Sundaes.

On these pages, you will find [Open] marking any establishment still in the Sundae business. If there is no sign, alas, the soda fountain is gone.

Still, many home refrigerators are stocked with ice creams and frozen yogurts that, with a dash of imagination, may become the basis for a Sundae when the yen hits.

Therefore, with a view to the past and a view to the present, I invite you to rediscover the grand, simple pleasure of a Sundae. Recipes require no special talent to implement, and most take only a few minutes to put together. I hope you will enjoy my book the way you might enjoy a Sundae (no, I don't mean diving to the bottom for the best part). Savor each section like components in a well-made Sundae, find your favorite flavors and textures, then come back for more.

And, please, if I haven't described your favorite Sundae or Sundae emporium, feel free to email me with details about it

–MICHAEL TURBACK
michael@icecreamsundae.com

TABLE OF CONTENTS

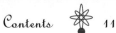

RECIPE GUIDE

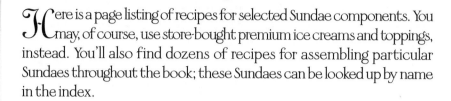

ℋere is a page listing of recipes for selected Sundae components. You may, of course, use store-bought premium ice creams and toppings, instead. You'll also find dozens of recipes for assembling particular Sundaes throughout the book; these Sundaes can be looked up by name in the index.

Chapter 1

PURSUIT OF HAPPINESS

"In matters of principle, stand like a rock;
in matters of taste, swim with the current."

–Thomas Jefferson

The happiness under consideration here rests on that most ephemeral of joys, ice cream. Chasing down the chef who first froze a dairy product is a pastime that leads to melting success. There are inklings that the concept may have been Himalayan and/or have originated in the gourmand minds of ancient Rome, where the heart of a dainty called *melca* appears to have been frozen milk. Long-ago Chinese emperors enjoyed a dessert of iced milk and rice; Indians still prepare a cold dairy dish of antique origin, *kulfi*.

Marco Polo is said to have noted something resembling iced milk in his travels and so sparked adaptations in the royal kitchens of Italy. When the exuberant Catherine de Mēdicis, only fourteen, arrived in France in 1533 to marry the Duke of Orleans, an ice cream recipe came with her.

Unadorned ice cream or *glacē* (in French) was on the menu of the Parisian bistro, Procope, when it was established in 1686, and it still is.

Ice cream was served in a few of the best homes in America not long afterward, if not before. Maryland governor William Bladen wrote of a dinner he'd enjoyed in 1700, "We had a dessert no less curious; among the rarities of which it was composed was some fine ice cream." He pronounced the dessert "delicious."

The first recorded American verdict on ice cream was in.

High-powered New Yorkers served naked ice cream in our country's first capital. George Washington enjoyed the dish during his initial presidential year, 1789, at the home of Alexander Hamilton. Whether this was Washington's first lick is unknown, but when he died, the Mount Vernon inventory included two pewter ice cream pots.

Thomas Jefferson is the founding father to whom we most owe our allegiance when it comes to establishing ice cream as a national dessert.

THOMAS JEFFERSON ESTABLISHED ICE CREAM AS THE NATIONAL DESSERT.

The moment our new ambassador set foot in Paris in 1784, he realized he was out of fashion in every way. To begin with, his Philadelphia-bought clothes were woefully *passé*. Averting disaster, he summoned a French haberdasher to properly adorn his six-foot, two-and-a-half-inch, long, thin frame with a bright blue waistcoat, jeweled hatband, pleated shirt with lace ruffles, satin breeches and, of course, knee buckles.

By and large, it didn't take Thomas Jefferson very long to make himself right at home on the Left Bank of the Seine. Political affairs would occupy much of his time, but this was also an opportunity for the omnivorous Virginian to navigate the cultural circles in Paris, including the culinary arts.

Jefferson was required to pay for most luxuries out of his own pocket. No matter; he owed it to the folks back home to hold his own among the Parisians. It cost him several hundred dollars to bring his accomplished

POLITICS & SUNDAES UPDATE I

If you or your spouse hope to be President of the United States, you can't campaign without a Sundae stop. New York Times columnist Maureen Dowd chronicled Elizabeth Dole's encounter with an ice cream Sundae at a New Hampshire Dairy Queen: "She let fly and ordered a cup of vanilla ice cream with hot fudge sauce and 'a little whipped cream and a lot of nuts.' She sat in a booth and stared down at the Sundae, teetering at the precipice of improvisation, perhaps recalling Jackie O's dictum: 'Never chew in camera range.'"

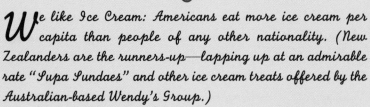

WHO LIKES ICE CREAM?

We like Ice Cream: Americans eat more ice cream per capita than people of any other nationality. (New Zealanders are the runners-up—lapping up at an admirable rate "Supa Sundaes" and other ice cream treats offered by the Australian-based Wendy's Group.)

The U.S. cities whose inhabitants eat the most ice cream are Portland (Oregon), St. Louis and Seattle. Ice cream purchases zoom up in July and August, and always on Sunday.

Ice cream is the number-one comfort food for both American men (27 percent) and women (23 percent). The good news is that ice cream, despite its fat content, has health benefits. Its calcium strengthens bones, its Vitamin A helps vision and its folic acid helps prevent birth defects.

And the good time extends beyond our taste buds. Eating ice cream produces brain chemicals like serotonin that elevate mood and lower blood pressure. It takes fifty bites to finish the average Sundae, and that's a lot of pleasure.

slave, James Hemings, from the States to Paris to learn the art of French cookery. After a shaky start, the ambassador's kitchen began turning out slow-cooked meats in wine-flavored ragouts. Macaroni (what we today would call spaghetti) was all the rage in Paris, so Chef Hemings also spent hours cutting dough into strips, then rolling it by hand into noodles.

Jefferson had two rules at his dinners: "No politics and no restraint." Guests were often surprised (and occasionally offended) by his practice of random seating, rather than traditional seating by rank. For dessert, Jefferson and his guests polished off *glacēs* as fast as the kitchen could send them out. Whenever he tasted French ice creams, Jefferson fell in love with Paris all over again.

In 1789, Jefferson agreed to relinquish his diplomatic post, and return to America as Secretary of State under George Washington. To stave off separation anxiety, he insisted on bringing his French butler, Adrien Petit, to Virginia along with Hemings. They were armed with a

POLITICS & SUNDAES UPDATE II

In his book, "Smashmouth," Washington Post reporter Dana Milbank, who covered the Al Gore 2000 campaign, explains that getting that Chocolate Sundae set before a Presidential candidate involves logistical planning: "You direct your 29-vehicle motorcade—two armored limousines, six vans, seven sedans, a dozen motorcycles, an ambulance, and a helicopter—to take you to [an Iowa] Dairy Queen. All 85 members of your entourage, including a bomb-sniffing dog and the man who carries the codes to launch nuclear missiles, descend on the ice cream shop. Police stop traffic, and security agents scurry about, speaking into microphones in their sleeves. As four photographers vie for position, you stroll to the counter to order your Chocolate Rock. Then you sit down to eat the confection and pretend not to notice that everybody in the place is staring at you."

ledger of standard French recipes—copied in Jefferson's own hand—including one for vanilla ice cream.

Almost immediately upon Jefferson's return to his hilltop farm, Monticello, ice cream appears in visitor accounts of meals with the author of our Declaration of Independence and future president. One dinner guest described a menu with "rice soup, round of beef, turkey, mutton, ham, loin of veal, cutlets of mutton or veal, fried eggs, fried beef, a pie called macaroni, and very good ice cream—a dish somewhat like pudding, covered with cream sauce—very fine."

Another visitor observed, "Among other things, ice-creams were produced in the form of balls of the frozen material inclosed [sic] in covers of warm pastry, exhibiting a curious contrast, as if the ice had just been taken from the oven."

Thomas Jefferson clearly had seized on the delightful notion of cold ice cream warmed by another flavor.

However, when grumpy Patrick Henry heard about the "foreign" foods being served at Jefferson's table—especially the extravagant desserts centering on ice cream—he protested that the Secretary of State had "abjured his native vittles." Jefferson considered the reproach "waggish," and he delighted in retelling the Patrick Henry story for years.

Vanilla remained Jefferson's favorite ice cream. His love of the flavor was so fervent that, while serving in the State Department, he wrote to the American envoy in Paris complaining about a lack of vanilla in the States, and requesting that fifty plump vanilla bean pods be sent to him at once. This request was made at the height of the French Revolution, while heads were rolling.

Jefferson was able to enjoy ice cream throughout most of the year because ice was harvested from the Rivanna River in winter and taken to Monticello's icehouse, which held sixty-two wagonloads. The icehouse, located in the estate's north dependency wing, had double walls built with heavy timbers, the gaps between them packed with sawdust. The stone floors were carpeted with sawdust on top of straw, and allowed for proper drainage. Insulation was so efficient that in 1815, Jefferson noted, his ice supply lasted all the way through mid-October.

Jefferson characteristically had his cooks combine the best of what he had eaten in Paris with the best that was one hundred percent American. During one particularly memorable dinner he hosted at Monticello, guests were served his finest vanilla ice cream bathed in maple syrup and accompanied by Savoy cookies.

Such a treat exemplified one aspect of the "pursuit of happiness" Jefferson had affirmed for his countrymen. And ice cream decked out with sauce and decorated with wafers was an intuitive herald of the Sundae yet to come.

THE RECIPES

HOMAGE TO JEFFERSON

*I*ce creams that use eggs are called either French-style ice creams or custards. What Thomas Jefferson would have loved most about this extremely rich custard ice cream is the flavor imparted by real vanilla bean pods and the thousands of minute seeds that show up as little black specks.

The seductively aromatic vanilla seeds infuse the ice cream with an elegant sweet note—soothing to the tongue and pleasing to the palate.

My preferred contemporary version of Jeffersonian ice cream requires a paring knife to unlock the vanilla bean's flavor, intensifying power. Carefully slit open the vanilla bean pod from end to end; this releases the concentrated flavor of the seeds. Your reward will be a rich, complex and indulgent dessert. You could try this classic French vanilla ice cream simply topped with pure maple syrup, to recreate the Jefferson party dessert, but I recommend adding warmth and crunch with maple-syrup bathed walnuts.

The guidance I offer below assumes you are using an electric ice cream maker. But any of the ice cream recipes in these pages can also be made (per manufacturer's instructions) in a hand-cranked machine. It will just take more time and a lot more effort.

FRENCH VANILLA BEAN ICE CREAM

3 large eggs	2 cups heavy cream
1 can (14 oz.) sweetened	2 cups half and half
condensed milk	Salt
1/4 cup brown sugar	1 vanilla bean pod

IN A LARGE MIXING BOWL, WHISK EGGS, CONDENSED MILK, BROWN SUGAR, HEAVY CREAM, HALF AND HALF AND A PINCH OF SALT. MIX THOROUGHLY AND TRANSFER TO LARGE SAUCEPAN. USE A PARING KNIFE TO SPLIT ONE LONG VANILLA BEAN POD LENGTHWISE AND CHOP INTO 1-INCH PIECES, THEN ADD THEM TO THE SAUCEPAN. HEAT THE MIX TO A LOW SIMMER WHILE STIRRING CONSTANTLY, AND CONTINUE TO SIMMER FOR ABOUT 15 MINUTES. STRAIN INTO A LARGE BOWL SO THAT THE LARGER PIECES OF POD ARE LEFT BEHIND. ALLOW MIXTURE TO COOL AND AGE IN THE REFRIGERATOR FOR ABOUT FOUR HOURS; THEN YOU ARE READY TO MAKE ICE CREAM.

WITH MY ICE CREAM MACHINE THERE IS A MIXING BOWL, WHICH HAS A SMALL ELECTRIC MOTOR AND A PLASTIC DASHER. THE PLASTIC BOWL IS LINED WITH A METAL RING FILLED WITH A LIQUID THAT, WHEN FROZEN, HOLDS COLD THROUGHOUT THE ICE CREAM-MAKING PROCESS. I PREFER TO FREEZE THE MIXING BOWL OVERNIGHT IN MY REFRIGERATOR FREEZER.

JUST POUR IN THE MIXTURE, TURN ON THE MACHINE, AND 30 MINUTES LATER YOU HAVE SOFT, CREAMY ICE CREAM. FOR SUNDAES, YOU WILL WANT THE

ICE CREAM A BIT FIRMER. JUST TRANSFER IT TO A CONTAINER AND PUT IT IN THE FREEZER FOR A FEW HOURS BEFORE SERVING.

WET WALNUTS

1 cup roughly chopped walnuts   *$^1/_4$ cup light corn syrup*
$^1/_4$ cup pure maple syrup

PREHEAT OVEN TO 350 DEGREES. SPREAD WALNUT PIECES ON A BAKING PAN IN A SINGLE LAYER. TOAST UNTIL GOLDEN BROWN AND FRAGRANT, ABOUT 10 MINUTES. REMOVE PAN FROM OVEN AND SET ASIDE. COMBINE PURE MAPLE SYRUP, CORN SYRUP AND WALNUTS IN A BOWL, THEN STIR UNTIL NUTS ARE WELL COATED. LADLE OVER THE ICE CREAM. MAKES 1 $^1/_2$ QUARTS OF ICE CREAM.

FRENCH CHOCOLATE ICE CREAM

*C*hocolate might be considered the ultimate American flavor, since cocoa is a New World plant, originating in Mexico. This ice cream is also "French" because it is a frozen egg custard. Chocolate ice creams did not become popular until the 1920s.

4 egg yolks   *2 cups half and half*
1 cup sugar   *1 cup heavy cream*
$^1/_3$ cup cocoa   *2 teaspoons real vanilla extract*

WHISK EGG YOLKS. GRADUALLY ADD SUGAR, THEN COCOA, HALF AND HALF, HEAVY CREAM AND VANILLA EXTRACT, CONTINUALLY WHISKING UNTIL THOROUGHLY BLENDED. FREEZE, FOLLOWING THE DIRECTIONS OF YOUR ICE CREAM-MAKING MACHINE. MAKES 1 $^1/_2$ QUARTS OF ICE CREAM.

Chapter 2

STRAWBERRY SURPRISES

"I doubt the world holds for anyone a more soul-stirring surprise than the first adventure with ice cream."

—HEYWOOD BROUN

adame Betty Jackson, an African-American woman with daring style, established a tearoom on French Street in Wilmington, Delaware, where she made homey cakes and pastries for high-society dinner parties. It was the early 1800s, and individual enterprise was afoot. Her hard-working son, Jeremiah Shadd, a butcher, saved enough money to purchase his wife Sallie's freedom, and she joined the family catering business. Sallie Shadd was a gifted confectioner who created a stir with her execution of a dessert she made from one of her mother-in-law's recipes, involving frozen cream, sugar and fresh fruit.

Dolley Madison, the adventurous wife of President James Madison, heard about Sallie's specialty, and journeyed to Wilmington to see and taste what all the fuss was about. Dolley was so impressed by Sallie's artful dome-molded ice creams in fruit colors that she imported Shadd's ideas to the White House, where they easily upstaged other desserts at State Dinners.

The array of ice creams Dolley Madison presented nearly upstaged the "Presidentress" herself, as the press dubbed her. Thomas Jefferson, who believed that women "should not wrinkle their foreheads with politics," was charmed by Dolley, as was nearly everyone else. In truth, although Dolley was chastised for meddling in government (as so many subsequent strong First Ladies have been), it was as a hostess that she made her indelible mark.

Vivacious and witty, Dolley quickened more than a few pulses in the capital and enlivened an otherwise dreary social scene. The founding mothers of America had little time for fashion, but Dolley seemed to have an intuitive gift for style. On the occasion of President Madison's second inaugural ball, the First Lady radiated from under a feathered turban. She wore a bright pink velvet creation with a square neck, strewn with flowers, and artfully tied with pink bows above a gathered, high-waisted slit skirt, worn over a tucked petticoat, "the color of crushed strawberries." according to one observer.

Her magnificent costume was matched only by the highlight of her grand buffet table: a strawberry ice-cream creation, molded to resemble Dolley's turban and of the same vivid pink as Dolley's gown. The ice cream was made of cream from the Madisons' dairy and strawberries fresh picked from their garden in Montpelier, Virginia. One guest described the moment: "When the brilliant assemblage entered the dining room, they beheld a table laden with good things to eat, and in the center, high on a silver platter, a large, shining dome of pink ice cream."

The great 20th-century chef and food writer, James Beard, laid America's love affair with ice cream at the feet of Washington's first brilliant hostess. He credited Dolley Madison with starting our "long-lived ice-cream binge."

A commercial "Dolly Madison" ice cream appeared in the 1950s, and is still produced by Cool Brands International in Ronkonkoma, New York.

Sallie Shadd's ice creams and others made in early 19th-century kitchens were made in pot freezers, also known by their French name, *sorbetiēres.* The ice cream mixture was placed in a bullet-shaped pewter pail, which was then set into a larger container holding four to six parts ice to one part rock salt, since salt lowers the freezing temperature of water. When salt is added to ice, the ice is forced to melt, drawing heat from its surroundings—in this case, the contents of the ice cream freezer. This chemical reaction cuts down appreciably on the time required for freezing.

A person churned and rocked

HAND CRANKING ICE CREAM WAS HARD WORK.

the outer container, stopping often to scrape the dairy mixture cling-ing to the interior sides of the pewter pot and stir it back in with a "spad-dle," a miniature spade with a long handle.

Making ice cream of an appealing texture was a finicky and exhausting business. If the ice cream in progress was too soft, that meant the brine was not cold enough, and more salt would be added to lower its temperature. If the ice cream was too coarse and icy, that indicat-ed the brine had become cold too quickly; too much salt had been used. Moreover, it took four to six hours of strong arm action and inside scrap-ing and stirring to make one pot of ice cream.

The toil of ice-cream making was somewhat eased in 1846, thanks to a New Jersey housewife named Nancy Johnson. The ingenious Mrs. Johnson came up with a design for a hand-cranked tin freezer that "automated" the scraping and blending in its interior can. One operated her device by turning a topside crank connected to an S-shaped dash-er in the freezer's interior drum. The dasher scraped ice crystals and kept the mixture in constant motion. This simultaneous freezing, scraping and stirring more efficiently incorporated air into the cream mixture, producing a smooth ice cream. It also required less ice in its outer drum than had the pot freezer, quite a boon in the days when ice had to be cut from a frozen lake, pond or river, hauled and conserved until sold or used.

Mrs. Johnson sold the patent for her invention to Williams & Company, a Philadelphia kitchen wholesaler, who by 1847 was selling ice cream makers at $3 each by the thousands. While generally it was only the menfolk who cut ice, the making of ice cream was one of the few activities that men, women and children shared. Whole families sociably gath-ered on porches around their ice-cream freezers, each per-son taking a turn at the crank. Some ice cream lovers prefer hand-cranked machines to this day, finding the resulting ice cream more honest than that created in electrical appliances. White Mountain Freezer started manufacturing human-powered

THIS ICE CREAM FREEZER WORKED WELL IF YOU WERE ENERGETIC AND LUCKY.

STEP LIVELY FOR ICE CREAM

*W*ell before the Civil War, America's most fashionable cities boasted ice cream "saloons," although the more refined term of "parlor" was also coming into use. Lee's Saloon in Boston served no spirits but dished up plenty of ice cream. Its dozens of round tables sat under candle chandeliers hanging from a ceiling at least thirty feet high. A band played on the balcony at the back of the large, elegant room. A lithograph of Lee's made when it was in full swing shows a room crowded by men in cutaways, a few accompanied by women in sweet bonnets or wearing bows and feathers in their hair.

Tunesmith J. R. Garcia loved this saloon so much that in 1841 he wrote a lively dance in its honor, "The Ice Cream Quick-Step." He dedicated the song to saloon owner William Lee as a "token of respect for [his] industry and enterprise."

ice cream freezers in 1872 in Laconia, New Hampshire, and still does—only now down in Nashua.

Nancy Johnson's cleverness liberated ice cream from the dining rooms of Presidents and others who could afford servants and brought it to the tables of common folks.

A few decades after the pleasure of ice cream had passed from the domains of the rich and famous to ordinary households, it also became a street-side familiar. The most successful street-sold ice cream of the 19th century was made by William A. Breyer. Unable to afford to rent a store from which to sell his products, Breyer hand-cranked ice creams in his home kitchen and peddled them from a horse-drawn wagon on the streets of Philadelphia. Breyer's ice cream grew more popular with each passing summer and, before his death in 1882, he had opened six retail stores.

His sons, Frederick and Henry, incorporated the business, expanded it into Philadelphia's suburbs and beyond, and developed the corporate logo featuring a sweetbrier leaf. The Breyers used pure, natural ingredients, limiting their formulas to milk, cream, sugar and natural flavorings,

ANOTHER PHILLY FIRST

🍒

*T*he very first ice cream soda was served in Philadelphia by sidewalk entrepreneur Robert M. Green. One of his more popular items was a slushy mixture of carbonated water, syrup, shaved ice and cream that he served to those visiting the Franklin Institute's 1874 science exposition. One day he ran out of cream and had to borrow ice cream from a neighboring concessionaire, which he planned to let melt before substituting it for the cream. However, when Green returned to his stand, he found several customers waiting impatiently. "With considerable anxiety," he much later recalled, he mixed a soda with the cream and served it. Thus was the ice-cream soda created, and it became an immediate sensation.

but eschewing egg yolks. This was genuine, native Philadelphia ice cream. Breyers still boasts "all natural" ice cream.

Although the milk and cream used to make ice cream contain natural stabilizers, some manufacturers in those early days of commercial production used additives such as arrowroot. It prevented the formation of large ice crystals in the ice creams and thereby increased smoothness. But too much arrowroot could spoil delicate flavors and result in a gummy texture.

Forget the notion of ice cream made with egg yolks—by the end of the 19th century, manufacturers who included eggs were accused of using additives!

Even commercial ice cream was created one batch at a time until 1925, when Clarence Vogt of Louisville, Kentucky, invented the "continuous-process freezer," which allowed the ice cream industry to become a mass-producer of its product.

GIVE ME THAT OLD TIME ICE CREAM

I learned how to make some of the very best homemade ice creams from my friend, Steve "Doc" Wilson of Fayetteville, Arkansas. He is the author of *Homemade Ice Cream: The Whole Scoop*, and his personal museum includes an amazing collection of ice cream scoops, milk shake mixers, advertisements, toys, drive-in trays and other manner of ice cream stuff.

Doc believes that ice cream is good medicine for a world where nothing is certain. "Notice that when a cold, sweet, refreshing bit of ice cream melts in your mouth, all your concerns melt away with it," says Doc. "Life, for one brief moment, is sweet, tranquil, and all is right with the world." His "Old Time Vanilla" does wonders for me. It's also the basis of my strawberry ice cream.

THE RECIPES

OLD TIME VANILLA ICE CREAM

2 eggs
1 can (14 ounces) sweetened
   condensed milk
$^1/_4$ cup sugar
$^1/_4$ cup brown sugar

2 cups heavy cream
2 cups half and half
Salt
$2^1/_2$ tablespoons pure vanilla
   extract

IN A LARGE MIXING BOWL, WHISK EGGS, ADD CONDENSED MILK AND WHISK TOGETHER UNTIL THOROUGHLY MIXED. ADD SUGAR AND BROWN SUGAR AND AGAIN MIX THOROUGHLY. THEN ADD HEAVY CREAM, HALF AND HALF, A PINCH OF SALT AND VANILLA EXTRACT. LET THE MIX CHILL IN THE REFRIGERATOR FOR ABOUT FOUR HOURS, WHICH ALLOWS THE MIXTURE TO AGE. THEN FREEZE, FOLLOWING THE DIRECTIONS OF YOUR ICE CREAM-MAKING MACHINE. MAKES 1 $^1/_2$ QUARTS OF ICE CREAM.

STRAWBERRY ICE CREAM

1½ quarts Old Time Vanilla mixture (refrigerated for 4 hours)
2 pints fresh, ripe strawberries

½ cup sugar
½ lemon
Red food color (optional)

CLEAN AND TOP THE STRAWBERRIES AND CUT THEM INTO BITE-SIZED PIECES. ADD SUGAR AND THE JUICE OF THE HALF LEMON. LET STRAWBERRIES MARINATE IN THE REFRIGERATOR OVERNIGHT OR AT LEAST 4 HOURS. WHEN THE OLD TIME VANILLA MIX HAS BEEN SUFFICIENTLY CHILLED AND IS READY FOR USE, STRAIN THE STRAWBERRIES, RESERVING THE JUICE. PLACE THE STRAW-BERRIES IN THE FREEZER COMPARTMENT OF YOUR REFRIGERATOR. COMBINE THE STRAWBERRY SYRUP AND VANILLA CREAM. IF YOU PREFER YOUR ICE CREAM PINK, ADD 10 DROPS OF THE FOOD COLOR. FREEZE THE ICE CREAM MIX, FOLLOWING THE RULES OF YOUR ICE CREAM MAKER. WHEN THE ICE CREAM IS ALMOST FROZEN, ADD THE STRAWBERRIES AND FINISH FREEZING.

REAL PHILADELPHIA VANILLA ICE CREAM

Egg yolks add to an ice cream's richness, but they also give the dessert a thickened texture, which causes some people palate fatigue by the third bite. By the end of the 19th century, the cleaner flavor of the Philadelphia-style concoction became the epitome of American ice cream. Any vanilla ice cream without egg yolks may fairly be called real Philadelphia. But I prefer to equate Philadelphia with getting down to ice cream basics.

This simple vanilla recipe provides an uncomplicated foundation for Sundae artistry.

---

2 cups heavy cream
1 cup milk

3/4 cup sugar
1 teaspoon vanilla extract

IN A LARGE MIXING BOWL COMBINE THE INGREDIENTS UNTIL WELL BLEND-ED. FREEZE, FOLLOWING THE INSTRUCTIONS OF YOUR ICE CREAM MACHINE. (TO MAKE A FRUIT ICE CREAM, ADD ½ CUP OF COARSELY CHOPPED FRUIT DURING THE LAST FEW MINUTES OF FREEZING). MAKES ONE QUART OF ICE CREAM.

STRAWBERRY ON TOP

"The strawberry, shaped by nature in conical form, is admirably adapted to topping a Sundae. It looks well and gives the customer an additional fillip. These little touches lend distinction to our service, scoring heavily in the aggregate." – DRUGGISTS CIRCULAR, JULY 1933

BREDENBECK'S SUNDAE

This luscious slice of American life owes something to Sallie Shadd for recognizing the affinity between ice cream and strawberries, something to Philly's vanilla ice cream tradition—in this case, Bassett's Philadelphia-made vanilla—and something to a recipe imported by a German immigrant.

Bredenbeck's was founded by Bavarian-born Frederick Robert Bredenbeck in 1889. A visit to this Chestnut Hill ice cream shop and bakery remains an after-dinner celebration.

DIP ONE LARGE SCOOP OF VANILLA ICE CREAM ONTO A SLICE OF BUTTER-POUND CAKE AND COVER WITH STRAWBERRY SYRUP. PLACE TWO WHOLE FRESH STRAWBERRIES ON THE TOP.

– BREDENBECK'S, PHILADELPHIA, PENNSYLVANIA

Chapter 3

BIRTH OF THE SUNDAE

"God put this game last, and it's just like putting a
cherry on top of your Sundae."

—GEORGIA TECH LINEMAN JONAS JENNINGS

The "Gay Nineties"—those were the days, my friend, and although they were over a century ago, their influence hasn't ended, not entirely.

In 1892, Benjamin Harrison, a five-foot-six, pot-bellied ex-Senator from Indiana, was in his final presidential year, having been elected with 100,000 fewer popular votes than Grover Cleveland. No matter, it was a patriotic era, and the band of John Philip Sousa was set to provide rousing marches for it. The Pledge of Allegiance was installed in public schools. The Immigrant Station at Ellis Island opened.

Ingenuity was everywhere. James Naismith, a young physical education instructor at Springfield College in Massachusetts, nailed two peach baskets to the balcony at either end of a gym and came up with thirteen rules for a new game: Basket Ball. Meanwhile, ten thousand fans at the Olympic Club in New Orleans watched James J. Corbett and John L. Sullivan put up their dukes—in innovative padded gloves—and slug it out for the heavyweight title.

The Duryea Brothers built the first American cars in 1892, and Alexander Graham Bell participated in the formal opening of long-distance telephone service between New York and Chicago. The zipper—introduced to fasten shoes—was patented. *Vogue* magazine debuted.

Spectacular crime ruled the headlines: Bob Ford, the "dirty little coward" who had shot Jesse James, was himself killed in a barroom brawl in Creede, Colorado. Back east, in Fall River, Massachusetts, Lizzie Borden dispatched her stepmother with an axe. Ninety minutes later, ditto her father.

But all was quiet in Ithaca, New York, a thriving college town at the southern tip of Cayuga Lake. The region was (and is) agricultural, but in

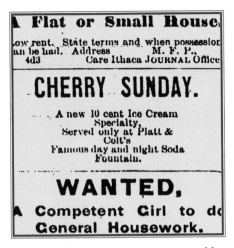

THE FIRST SUNDAE WAS ADVERTISED ON MAY 28, 1892 IN THE DAILY JOURNAL, ITHACA, N.Y.

Ithaca two very American manufacturers flourished: Ithaca Gun and the Ithaca Calendar Clock Company.

On Saturdays, particularly, people shopped downtown at Rothschild's "Boston-style" department store to the clang of its new mechanical cash register and, far above Cayuga's waters, Cornell University students rode those new "safety" bicycles, the ones with two wheels of the same size and air-filled tires. A popular stop was one of the neighborhood drugstore soda fountains, where many a nickel was spent for a dish of ice cream.

On Sundays, most people went to church, but even then Ithaca was a town with some tolerance for those who didn't.

The Reverend John M. Scott delivered a sermon at the Unitarian Church one fine April Sunday morning. Finding himself at loose ends that afternoon, he paid a visit to the Platt & Colt Pharmacy on State Street, where his friend, the drugstore proprietor Chester Platt, presided. History—Sundae history!—was about to be made, although it's doubtful that either gentleman recognized the full importance of what would momentarily take place. Within days, Platt was advertising his discovery—the "Sunday"—in the local newspaper.

Decades later, when the time and place of the invention of the Sundae had become a matter of some dispute, DeForest Christiance, the Platt & Colt clerk who had witnessed the event, offered his testimony. Notice that Christiance does not claim credit for himself (making his version all the more credible) in the letter he wrote to local historian and Ithaca librarian, John G. Brooks, describing the momentous occasion:

About the much discussed origin of the ice cream concoction called Sunday, Sundae and Sundi; About 45 years ago, on a Sunday afternoon, John M. Scott, then pastor of the Unitarian Church, and Chester Platt were having their usual Sunday confab in back of the prescription counter, when Mr. Platt proposed that they have some refreshment. Mr. Platt then came up to the soda fountain, where I was holding forth, asking for two dishes of ice cream, and on each he placed a candied cherry, then, after considering a bit, he poured cherry syrup over them, making a very attractive looking dessert.

When he and Mr. Scott tried out this new concoction, they became very enthusiastic about its flavor and appearance, and immediately started casting about for a suitable name. It was then that Mr. Scott said why not call it Cherry Sunday in com-memoration of the day on which it was invented. This name appealed to Mr. Platt, so from that day on we served Cherry Sunday, and later on Strawberry, Pineapple, Chocolate, etc.

—DeForest Christiance, May 25, 1936

There you have it—ice cream with syrup and a cherry on top, named after its day of birth—the original Sundae! The creation began with one small scoop for man but soon became accepted as one giant gift to mankind.

Humble Chester Platt could not have foreseen himself as the Neil Armstrong of Planet Ice Cream, but he and the Rev. Scott had recognized a good thing when they'd tasted it. Platt advertised the "Cherry Sunday" in the Ithaca *Daily Journal* issue of April 5, 1892. A few days later, the paper ran a brief describing the ice cream novelty, which it said was topped with "cherry juice syrup" and "candied French cherries" and served in a champagne glass.

Platt and Christiance were astute enough to repeat the success. Soon, they concocted a prototype strawberry "Sunday" and Platt advertised that dish in the local newspaper, too.

A few citizens may have been shocked to learn that a spectacular indulgence was named after the Sabbath, but it was the delight not the irreverence that made the stir. And Ithaca is not so much changed today. Only a few years ago, Jon Spayde wrote in the bi-monthly, *Utne Reader,* "Ithaca, N.Y., is the most politically correct and spiritually aware and pro-gressively enlightened place in the United States."

The invention of the Sundae rapidly became a national affair, as Cornell men on school vacations carried with them to their hometowns,

PURITY IS A VIRTUE

Today, Ithaca has its share of franchised Sundaes but the Purity Ice Cream Company is the town's leading maker and purveyor of premium ice cream. The company was started back in 1936 by one of those Cornell fellers with a sweet tooth. Leo Guentert thought he could make a better chocolate ice cream and he was right. Purity is owned now by Bruce and Heather Lane who mix and package several Purity flavors in relatively small batches to keep the local legend going strong.

far and wide, requests that soda fountains copy the treats they'd discovered in Ithaca town.

If you stop and think about it, the American Ice Cream Sundae had been on the verge of invention since the days of Thomas Jefferson and Dolley Madison. Jefferson had ladled maple syrup on ice cream; Madison had served Sallie Shadd's ice cream and strawberry creation to thousands of trendsetters. Yet it was not until one crystalline moment

A DRUGSTRORE FOUNTIAN, CIRCA 1900.

in 1892 that it all came together, and the Sundae was born and baptized, and very soon thereafter offered for public consumption, right up to the cherry on top.

EDUCATED TASTES

*D*own in University Park, Pennsylvania, an ice cream fountain has been part of the Penn State curriculum since 1896. While only some students apply themselves to the science of ice cream making, almost all gain from it—literally. The fountain is famous for its super-rich ice creams, and at Penn State the "freshmen five," the extra pounds most first-year college students are said to put on, thanks to institutional food, translates to the "freshmen ten or twenty." By their sophomore year, most Penn State kids have learned to cut back, take up running or switch to frozen yogurt.

Cornell University boasts a Dairy Store, operated by the Department of Food Science where, fittingly, Sundae variations are popular. Semesters open with new treats, such as Mexican Sundae Ice Cream (vanilla with incorporated dark chocolate flakes and Spanish peanuts). For gala events, a red and white hometown invention, the Strawberry Sundae, reigns. At a recent commencement, 10,000 Strawberry Sundaes, matching the university colors, were served.

THE RECIPES

EASY CHOCOLATE ICE CREAM

This recipe can be made into double-chocolate ice cream by stirring in ³/₄ cup of semisweet chocolate mini-chips ten or fifteen minutes before ice cream freezing time is over.

2 cups heavy cream　　　　　　　*¹/₂ cup chocolate syrup*
1 cup milk

IN A LARGE MIXING BOWL COMBINE THE INGREDIENTS IN THE ORDER LISTED UNTIL WELL BLENDED. FREEZE, FOLLOWING THE INSTRUCTIONS OF YOUR ICE CREAM MACHINE. MAKES ONE QUART OF ICE CREAM.

CANDIED CHERRIES

Because the cherry has distinctively marked most Sundaes since that very first one, you might wish to candy your own. If you'd also like to give your Sundae cherries an alcoholic kick, add ¹/₄ cup of cherry liqueur or cherry kirsch at the end of cooking. It's highly unlikely, though, that the Platt & Colt cherry on the Cherry Sundae contained a whisper of alcohol.

1 pound fresh cherries, stemmed　　*¹/₂ cup water*
and pitted　　　　　　　　　　　*¹/₂ lemon*
2 cups sugar　　　　　　　　　　*1 cup apple juice*

BRING THE SUGAR AND WATER TO A BOIL IN A MEDIUM-SIZE HEAVY SAUCEPAN. ADD THE CHERRIES AND THE LEMON HALF. REDUCE THE HEAT TO A SIMMER AND COOK UNTIL THE SYRUP IS RED AND SLIGHTLY THICK, OR ABOUT 20 MINUTES. COVER AND LET STAND FOR 3 TO 4 HOURS, OR OVERNIGHT.

STRAIN THE CHERRIES, RESERVING THE SYRUP, AND SET CHERRIES ASIDE. DISCARD THE LEMON HALF AND ADD THE APPLE JUICE TO THE SYRUP. BRING THE SYRUP TO A HARD BOIL AND COOK FOR 5 MINUTES. RETURN THE CHERRIES TO THE SYRUP, REDUCE THE HEAT AND COOK SLOWLY UNTIL THE SYRUP IS THICK (TO ABOUT 220 DEGREES IF YOU ARE USING A CANDY THERMOMETER). REMOVE FROM HEAT AND LET COOL. MAKES ENOUGH TO TOP A DOZEN OR SO SUNDAES.

CLASSIC STRAWBERRY DELIGHT

Strawberry syrup is best made when strawberries are in season. Use frozen berries if you must. This syrup, chilled or at room temperature and poured over vanilla ice cream, is a dessert in itself. But you certainly may add freshly whipped cream, with a cherry (or, for that matter, a whole fresh strawberry) on top.

2 quarts fresh, sweet strawber-ries	*1 cup sugar (a little more if berries are tart)*

WASH, STEM AND CRUSH BERRIES, USING A POTATO MASHER OR FORK, AND CRUST LIGHTLY WITH SUGAR. LET SET FOR AT LEAST AN HOUR TO ALLOW BERRIES TO MACERATE AND RELEASE THEIR JUICE. TRANSFER SWEETENED BERRIES AND JUICE TO A LARGE, HEAVY SAUCEPAN AND CAREFULLY BRING TO A SIMMER. COOK, STIRRING OFTEN, FOR ABOUT 12 TO 15 MINUTES OR UNTIL SLIGHTLY THICKENED.

CHERRY SUNDAE

An honest cherry Sundae is hard to find today. My favorite version is simply made by spooning chunky cherry preserves over vanilla ice cream. Or you can top chocolate ice cream with the preserves and then ladle chocolate syrup over it for a Black Forest Sundae. Another easy model comes from the Southwest and has over a half-century of experience behind it.

DIP ONE LARGE SCOOP OF VANILLA ICE CREAM INTO A SUNDAE TULIP. COVER THE ICE CREAM WITH A LADLEFUL OF BORDEAUX CHERRIES IN SYRUP, GARNISH WITH WHIPPED CREAM, AND PLACE A SINGLE CHERRY AT THE TOP.

– MODEL PHARMACY, ALBUQUERQUE, NEW MEXICO

ABC SUNDAE

My enlightened hometown is a pioneer in the subspecies crunchy-granola Sundae. At one coffeehouse, you can hear music on

Saturday night, then return for a macrobiotic Sunday dinner, followed by a dessert that improbably incorporates a Jeffersonian ice cream tradition with "health-food" munchies.

• •

DIP TWO LARGE SCOOPS OF VANILLA ICE CREAM IN A LARGE SOUP BOWL. SPRINKLE TWO OUNCES OF GRANOLA OVER THE TOP, FOLLOWED BY DRIZZLES OF BOTH CHOCOLATE AND MAPLE SYRUPS. GARNISH WITH FRESHLY WHIPPED CREAM.

• •

- ABC CAFĒ, ITHACA, NEW YORK

Chapter 4

THE GREAT PRETENDERS

"The crushed strawberries of ice cream soda places,
the night wind in the cottonwoods and willows,
the lattice shadows of doorsteps and porches,
these know more of the story."

–CARL SANDBURG, *CORNHUSK*

enry Louis Mencken, the cranky Baltimore newspaperman with a cigar perpetually jammed in the side of his mouth, once suggested that mankind's chief occupation is believing passionately what is palpably not true. He hated the Ice Cream Sundae. He called the "misspelled" dessert a "soda-fountain mess," and concluded that it was precisely the strange spelling that was responsible for its popularity.

Two Rivers, Wisconsin, a port city on Lake Michigan—on 15th Street to be exact—is where Mencken placed the blame for Sundaes. In his first volume of *The American Language*, published in 1919, he wrote that a customer named George Hallauer urged Edward C. Berners, owner of

---

ONLY ON SUNDAY

In "Origins", his etymological dictionary, Eric Partridge informs us that the Ice Cream Sundae doubtless derives from the word Sunday, perhaps because "an ordinary ice cream was good enough for a weekday, [but] only this special kind was good enough for a Sunday."

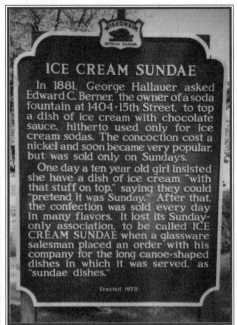

ICE CREAM SUNDAE

In 1881, George Hallauer asked Edward C. Berner, the owner of a soda fountain at 1404-15th Street, to top a dish of ice cream with chocolate sauce, hitherto used only for ice cream sodas. The concoction cost a nickel and soon became very popular, but was sold only on Sundays.

One day a ten year old girl insisted she have a dish of ice cream "with that stuff on top," saying they could "pretend it was Sunday." After that, the confection was sold every day in many flavors. It lost its Sunday-only association, to be called ICE CREAM SUNDAE when a glassware salesman placed an order with his company for the long canoe-shaped dishes in which it was served, as "sundae dishes."

Erected 1973

ICE CREAM SUNDAE MARKER IN TWO RIVERS, WI.

the town's ice cream parlor, to top a dish of ice cream with the chocolate sauce Berners used for ice cream sodas. Berners warned that it would ruin the ice cream, but Hallauer ordered it anyway. This is said to have occurred on July 7, 1881. Sometime later, on a weekday, a ten-year-old girl requested a dish of ice cream "with that stuff on top," pleading with the soda jerk to "pretend it was Sunday."

But how do the history-minded people of Two Rivers know all this? They read the plaque in the town's central park, which was put up in 1973! Fifty-four years after H.L. Mencken's mocking account, some Two Rivers citizens decided to go along with it—sort of. So little respect was shown for "the first Sundae" claim that the building that had housed Berners' was torn down in 1979. Walter Vogel, president of the Two Rivers Historical Society, acknowledges that the Mencken story is the basis for the town's first-Sundae belief.

Now it could be that Edward C. Berners of Two Rivers served up the first Sundae with chocolate sauce, but when? Why didn't the Wisconsin town circulate news of the discovery some allege? If you give Two Rivers the benefit of the broadest doubt and say, yes, some chocolate syrup got splashed on some ice cream there unfashionably early, then you come to a profound question: If a metal spoon clicks against a glass dish and nobody hears it, is that the noise of a Sundae?

Whether you're philosophical or not, it's possible to see *a replica* of Berners' Ice Cream Parlor in Two Rivers' Washington House Museum; over eighteen different sorts of Sundaes are offered there, several of them awfully good, I'm told.

I'm for the propagation of Sundae culture wherever. But I still say the Cherry Sundae devised at Platt & Colt in Ithaca was the very *first*

Sundae. And while I admit that the Cherry Sundae has not maintained its hold on America the way the chocolate-sauced Sundae has, the Strawberry Sundae, also conceived at Platt & Colt, certainly has had a long run.

Since I'm sitting here writing confessions, I'll acknowledge that I'm a partisan. I'm an Ithacan, and if Platt & Colt's cherry-red colors my views, so be it.

Another Wisconsin town, suspiciously near Two Rivers, also has claimed to be the town where Sundaes were invented. That town is Manitowoc, where the best-selling ice cream at George Giffy's soda fountain was plain vanilla. One day, in Manitowoc's version, a little girl asked Giffy to pour the chocolate syrup, reserved for chocolate soda, over her nickel portion of vanilla. Giffy obliged but charged five cents extra.

A dime ice-cream dish was too expensive for workdays, but Giffy thought the dressed-up crowd who patronized his establishment after church might go for it. He also decided to name his dish for Sunday—but with a twist. Maybe he was afraid of sacrilege or maybe he was just seized with the same sort of disrespect for English that causes the owner of a cheap cabaret to put up a sign that reads, "Nite Club." Whatever his thinking, Giffy called his sauced ice cream a "Sundae." And where, I ask you, was the cherry on top?

Mencken had such a good time inventing a rivalry between Two Rivers and Manitowoc that he missed the real point: Much better evidence points to Ithaca as the Sundae's hometown. Mencken got it hilariously wrong but decades later the American "newspaper of record" got it right. In *The New York Times Food Encyclopedia* (1985), Craig Claiborne certified Ithaca as birthplace of the Sundae.

Other locales entertain their own delusions of Sundae grandeur. In Buffalo, New York, mighty fine Sundaes are served to this day, but some

---

A SEASON WITHOUT A SUNDAE

❦

"*Watching other teams in the World Series is like watching someone else eat a Hot Fudge Sundae.*"
—JOE TORRE, MANAGER, NEW YORK YANKEES

locals would also like to buffalo you into thinking that their city is where it all began. Their hometown legend traces back to Stoddard Brothers, the first Buffalo drugstore to install a soda fountain, selling ice cream sodas for a nickel—that is, until the day the store ran out of soda water. Uncle Charley Stoddard needed to whistle up a new dish in a hurry, so he instructed his clerks to serve two scoops of ice cream drenched with fruit syrup. Conveniently, no one attributes an exact year to this proto-Sundae. Charley's idea stuck in Buffalo, and so, I might add, did the myth that Uncle Charley was the first person to even pour syrup on ice cream. Tell *that* to Jefferson scholars.

We also have the curious case of Norfolk, Virginia, trying to turn its intolerant past into something good. In the late 19th century, Norfolk's blue laws prohibited the sale of both alcohol and *soda* on the Sabbath. To circumvent the restriction, it is purported that a clever fountain owner added a few berries, fruit syrup and ice cream to an ice cream soda glass, but held off on the fizzy water.

America's greatest dessert, some Virginians claim, came into being as a legal subterfuge. A "dry" ice cream soda became a Sundae. Not only does this raffish explanation tarnish the rep of a Sundae, it depends on our going along with the notion that the original Sundae arrived with what—a blueberry?—on top.

Evanston, Illinois, Chicago's neighbor, also submits a claim to having cradled the Sundae for much the same reason as Norfolk. But Evanston's brief gives me more pause. Evanston was the town that helped shape and was later shaped by 19th-century Women's Christian Temperance Union leader Frances Willard. The puritanical fervor of this town, nicknamed "Heavenston," resulted in a town without saloons, where not a moment of Sunday was to be spent in idle pleasure. Children's swings were chained still and stern Methodist clergy insisted that those hedonistic intoxicants served in soda fountains—the ones loaded with sugar and all those bubbles—might bring out the devil in an unsuspecting soul. Ice cream sodas were strictly a never-on-Sunday indulgence.

The assertion that the Sundae was actually *invented* in Evanston was put forth years ago, but even on that windy shore it could never have had many subscribers. In 1939, *The Evanston Daily News* allowed that a local youth who had attended Cornell might have brought the Sundae concept home with him. But then again, the writer reasoned, a Northwestern student might have transported his Sundae habit to Ithaca.

The commentator did not explain how a boy who attended

"*THEY'LL DO IT EVERY TIME!*"

Northwestern University, which of course is in Evanston, would have acquired the jones for Sundaes. This same writer erred in asserting that the Sundae debuted in Ithaca in 1897, and this mistake leaves five years for the Sundae to have reached Evanston. In Sundae time, half a decade is an eon. The Ithaca Sundae was so brilliant that news of it zipped from coast to coast in mere months, without the help of air travel, television or e-mail.

"Legends have a way of growing until they become accepted as true stories," admits Kim Olsen-Clark, archivist for the Evanston Historical Society.

Evanston, however, has a stronger case for having been instrumental in changing the dessert's spelling. Because, without doubt, it offended local leaders of the faith that the name of the Lord's Day had become affixed to something sweet and gooey. Pulpits rang with denunciations of "the Sunday," and it came to pass that wherever that offering appeared on a local menu, it was spelled "Sundae."

The gentleman who came up with this peace offering might have been William C. Garwood, proprietor of the Evanston drugstore that bore his name. Garwood, for sure, had a clever streak; he also may have introduced curbside service to our great nation. He installed an electric bell outside his establishment at the right height for carriage drivers to ring it as a summons. An answering waiter would take the order of passengers and deliver it to them either in their carriage or under a nearby shade tree.

The final competitor in the Sundae-invention sweepstakes is the Illinois town of Plainfield. Once more, the story goes, a hapless druggist, a man whose surname was Sonntag, was only trying to make a demanding patron happy. After dressing a dish of ice cream with syrup, the druggist decided to feed his ego by naming the new dish after himself. Sonntag means Sunday in German, and you already know the rest.

THE RECIPES

CLASSIC CHOCOLATE SYRUP

6 ounces semi-sweet chocolate $^1/_4$ cup water
$^1/_2$ cup evaporated milk

MELT CHOCOLATE IN TOP OF A DOUBLE BOILER. GRADUALLY STIR IN EVAPORATED MILK, AND CONTINUE STIRRING UNTIL SAUCE IS FULLY BLENDED AND SMOOTH. REMOVE FROM HEAT AND STIR IN WATER UNTIL SMOOTH. MAKES 1 CUP.

SYRUP MAY BE REFRIGERATED IN AN AIRTIGHT CONTAINER FOR UP TO 3 WEEKS. TO REHEAT, SET OVER A DOUBLE BOILER AND STIR UNTIL SMOOTH. IF RE-HEATING OVER DIRECT HEAT, USE VERY LOW FLAME, AND BE CAREFUL NOT TO LET THE SAUCE BUBBLE OR BURN.

WASHINGTON HOUSE SUNDAE

$\mathcal{T}$he sentiment is obvious in this patriotic creation made with red, white and blue ice creams. The red is strawberry, the white is vanilla, and the blue is pistachio with a little help from food color.

DIP ONE LARGE SCOOP EACH OF STRAWBERRY, VANILLA AND BLUE PISTACHIO INTO A TALL SUNDAE GOBLET LINED WITH CHOCOLATE SYRUP. COVER THE ICE CREAMS WITH CRUSHED STRAWBERRIES, CRUSHED PINEAPPLE, AND MARSH-MALLOW SYRUP. GARNISH WITH WHIPPED CREAM, AND PLACE A MARASCHINO CHERRY AT THE TOP.

– BERNERS' ICE CREAM PARLOR, TWO RIVERS, WISCONSIN

HARD HAT SUNDAE

$\mathcal{I}$f you make this at home, use a new hat and line it with foil or waxed paper. Or finish this Sundae at Beernsten's and you get to keep the hard hat.

SELECT 10 LARGE SCOOPS OF ICE CREAM AND PLACE IN CONSTRUCTION HAT. ADD CHOICE OF 5 SUNDAE TOPPINGS, GARNISH WITH WHIPPED CREAM, AND PLACE FIVE CHERRIES AT THE TOP.

– BEERNSTEN'S CONFECTIONARY, MANITOWOC, WISCONSIN

CO-ED SUNDAE

INTO A WIDE SUNDAE DISH, PLACE 2 LARGE SCOOPS OF VANILLA ICE CREAM OVER A SLICED BANANA. COVER THE ICE CREAM WITH HOT FUDGE SAUCE, GARNISH WITH WHIPPED CREAM, AND PLACE 2 MARASCHINO CHERRIES ON TOP.

– DOUMAR'S, NORFOLK, VIRGINIA

Chapter 5

SPLIT PERSONALITIES

🍒

Time flies like an arrow. Fruit flies like a banana."

– GROUCHO MARX

The boardwalk of Atlantic City was the solution to the mess of hotel guests tracking sand on the carpets. By the turn of the last century, planks forty feet wide stretched for four miles above the beach. This boardwalk was dotted with stalls and stands offering everything imaginable to "lick, chew, munch, gulp or swill," in the words of optometrist David Strickler of Latrobe, Pennsylvania, who vacationed in Atlantic City in the summer of '04. Only eight years after the miracle in Ithaca, Sundaes were big in Atlantic City.

Watching the soda jerks at Gage's Ice Cream Parlor on the boardwalk hawking Sundaes topped with nuts, fresh fruits and a variety of syrups, Strickler was inspired to create his own masterwork. Back home in Latrobe, he started experimenting at the soda fountain in his

PHOTO BY TOM VANO.

MUSICAL TRIBUTE

*L*ouis Prima and his up-tempo band packed them into Vegas' 120-seat Casbar Lounge in the Sahara Hotel. His audiences included headliner Frank Sinatra and the Rat Pack entourage, Howard Hughes with his starlet of the moment, and a young Massachusetts senator named John F. Kennedy. In 1956, Prima rocked the joint with "Banana Split for My Baby."

BANANA SPLIT FOR MY BABY

Banana Split for my baby
And a glass of plain water for me.
Banana Split for my baby
And a glass of plain water for me.

Dispenser man, if you please
Serve my chick a mess of calories.
Banana Split for my baby
And a glass of plain water for me.

Flip back the lid, flip everything
  sight
Make it a rainbow of red, brown
  and white.
Chocolate chip and everything that's
  nice
Tutti fruiti once, and spumoni
  twice.

Spray the whipped cream for at
  least an hour
Pile it as high as the Eiffel Tower.
Load it with nuts, about sixteen
  tons
Top it with a pizza just for fun.

Stack her up with crazy goo
'Cause that's the stuff she likes to
wade right through.
Banana Split for my baby
And a glass of plain water for me.

Now add the cherries, the kind she
  loves to munch
Skip one banana, use the whole
  darn bunch
Drown it in fudge, six or seven cans
Give her two spoons, she'll eat
  with both hands.

Separate checks, it must be
Charge the split to her, the water to
me.
Oh, the Banana Split's for my
  baby
And the glass of plain water's for
me.
(Ain't got no money)
The glass of plain water's for me.

pharmacy. The line of inquiry that interested him was how to incorporate into a Sundae the yellow tropical fruit that was now being shipped up north from the port of New Orleans.

Never for a moment did Strickler doubt the possibilities of a banana. With a display of originality, he sliced it down the middle for easier eating and made the long halves the bed of an invention he called the Banana Split Sundae.

The new dessert was a symphony of delight: each of its movements poised to satisfy the popular sweet tooth, the whole a crescendo of pleasure. Three scoops of different-flavored ice creams were heaped on the sliced bananas; all was then enveloped by strawberries, raspberries and crushed pineapple. Strickler, the Toscanini of Sundaes, added marshmallow syrup and sprinkled on chopped nuts. Finally, he perched pitted black cherries atop each mound.

Strickler sold this extravaganza for a mere ten cents. It was a truly flabbergasting Sundae, and the students at nearby St. Vincent's College went (how else to put it?) bananas.

But Stricker was not yet satisfied. He needed a way to display his horizontal Sundae so that its visual appeal would be a match for his note-by-note construction. So he persuaded the Westmoreland Glass Company in nearby Grapeville to press the world's first banana-split boats. Soon, Westmoreland was selling its long, horizontal glass bowls for $1.50 a dozen.

Americans found the banana split irresistible—quite possibly because it erased some of the agonizing decisions inherent in ordering a simpler Sundae: What flavor ice cream? What sort of sauce? Which fruit? Bananas were compatible with everything, it seemed. This was a clear case of *more is more*.

Gus Napoulos was splitting bananas at the Elite Confectionery in Davenport, Iowa, by 1906. Folks in Wilmington, Ohio, first ate Ernest Hazard's banana splits during the blustery winter of 1907. And Letty Lally offered an early banana-and-ice cream concoction at the soda fountain of Foeller's Drug Store in nearby Columbus that same year.

Others ran their own variations on Strickler's theme. Stinson Thomas, head soda fountain clerk at Butler's Department Store in Boston, devised a banana split that included a banana sliced lengthwise and topped with two small scoops of vanilla ice cream, each topped with a cherry. A few slices of peach, a bit of pistachio and crushed walnuts finished it off.

But it was an ambitious Chicago pharmacist who secured the banana split's place in American culinary culture.

In 1901, Charles Walgreen borrowed $2,000 from his father for a

TRIPLE THE FUN

🍒

"Suppose we do a number with musical swords and we can end up cutting Honey in half?" —Fred (Fred Astaire)

"I'd much rather split a Banana Split three ways." —Honey (Ginger Rogers)

- FLYING DOWN TO RIO

down payment on his first drugstore. The slim young man in his twenties opened his store at 7:30 in the morning and rarely left before 11 at night. Only once in a great while did he take a few hours off in the afternoon to watch the White Sox play ball. After eight hardscrabble years, Walgreen sold a half interest in his store to open a second location, where he installed a sixteen-foot-long, marble-top soda fountain, plus eight small tables and six booths.

Walgreen, who churned ice cream in the basement of this store, dressed his clerks in crisp white uniforms with black bow ties to serve phosphates, Sundaes and banana splits. By 1916, there were nine Walgreen drugstores, by 1919 eleven more. To meet the demand for ice cream, Walgreen established his own manufacturing plant.

Walgreen's Banana Split Sundae nearly duplicated Doc Strickler's original, and the fountain managers at each Walgreen location remained true to it. Not all its soda jerks cooperated, however. In 1926, Lucille Ball worked the fountain at a Walgreen's in Jamestown, New York. Her tenure was brief. "I was fired," she told friends, "for forgetting to put the banana in a banana split!"

By the end of 1929, there were 397 Walgreens in 87 cities, and the banana split had become practically synonymous with the drug-store chain.

Strickler's creation weathered the Depression, and the banana split became a benchmark for impressing dates for years to come.

A young but already successful Elvis Presley was high enough on banana splits and other Sundaes to consider them date fare, but toward his end his enthusiasm had warped into a bloated and lonely affair; his downing of as many as five for breakfast could not push away his demons.

Recent decades, however, have not been kind to the banana split. There are over 3,000 Walgreen pharmacies in the United States, but not one soda fountain remains. Today finds the typical Walgreen's in a mall. When Americans took to their cars in the 1950s, '60s and '70s and headed to shopping centers to load up on groceries, drugs and almost

HARD ROCK WAY OR WALGREEN'S WAY?

🍒

Most boardwalk soda jerks are long gone, perhaps to become croupiers. But you can still get a pretty good banana split in Atlantic City, although now you'll have to visit the Hard Rock Café. Of course, if you come from another tourist town, you may already know the Hard Rock split. It's a mighty fair rendition of the classic, with three scoops of vanilla, dressed with a trio of sauces (strawberry, pineapple, and chocolate), sided with banana slices, topped with fresh whipped cream and sprinkled with chopped Brazil nuts and chocolate jimmies. It's served straight up in an oversized martini glass with a single cherry at the top.

Or you can follow Walgreen's original 9-step program to banana split perfection:

1. Peel a fresh banana and split it in two the long way.
2. Line up the halves at the bottom of a special glass dish.
3. Add one scoop each of vanilla, chocolate and strawberry ice cream.
4. Cover with crushed pineapple, chocolate syrup and fresh strawberries.
5. Put a big burst of whipped cream on each scoop.
6. Sprinkle with chopped nuts and chocolate bark shavings.
7. Top off the entire concoction with three stemmed maraschino cherries.
8. Put two Nabisco™ wafers at either end.
9. Serve with a long-handled spoon.

– WALGREEN'S ORIGINAL INSTRUCTIONS

everything else they regularly needed, they left many of Main Street's leisurely pleasures behind.

Not that the banana split has gone the way of the dodo bird; it's still available for those with time and spirit enough to indulge. But even teenagers are harried today, prepping for their SAT tests and worrying about their figures to the point of anorexia. They have social lives, of course, but what constitutes a good time has also changed somewhat. These days, high school couples don't split off for a split. If two even pair off from the gang with whom they "hang," it's possibly to "hook up" in some more private way. Or like yuppies, they steal away to a coffee bar, which probably has a half-dozen trendy names for ice cream-laced drinks, and there they sip their dessert rather than slowly spooning it from a banana boat.

Still, there are times when only a banana split is a match for a lusty appetite. In this health-conscious era, many people theoretically agree that the average banana split is big enough for two. But in practice, it's understandable that not everyone wants to share.

THE RECIPES

WINNING WHIPPED CREAM

To make the best whipped cream for Sundaes and Banana Splits, use heavy cream with a butterfat content between 30% and 40%. The richer the cream, the more air it will trap and hold. Use a well-chilled bowl (I chill both bowl and beater in the freezer ahead of time). Most recipes call for confectioner's sugar, but I prefer to use sweetened condensed milk, which makes a more stable whipped cream.

•••

1 cup heavy cream   *¹/₄ cup sweetened condensed milk*

•••

COMBINE HEAVY WHIPPING CREAM AND CONDENSED MILK (BOTH WELL-CHILLED) IN A METAL MIXING BOWL. WHIP WITH A HAND-HELD ELECTRIC MIXER AT MEDIUM-HIGH SPEED. TO INCORPORATE THE MOST AIR, MOVE THE BEATERS UP, DOWN, AND AROUND THE SIDES OF THE BOWL DURING WHIPPING. WHEN THE CREAM HAS DOUBLED IN VOLUME AND FORMS STIFF PEAKS, YOU ARE READY TO GARNISH YOUR SUNDAES.

FLUFFY MARSHMALLOW SAUCE

2 large egg whites	*16 regular marshmallows*
1 cup sugar	*¹/₄ teaspoon vanilla extract*
¹/₂ cup water	

USING AN ELECTRIC MIXER, BEAT EGG WHITES IN A MIXING BOWL ON MEDIUM SPEED UNTIL SOFT PEAKS FORM, ABOUT 2-3 MINUTES. SET ASIDE. COMBINE SUGAR AND WATER IN A MEDIUM-SIZE SAUCEPAN AND PLACE OVER MEDIUM HEAT. STIR UNTIL SUGAR DISSOLVES. STOP STIRRING AND ALLOW SUGAR/WATER MIXTURE TO COME TO A BOIL. BOIL FOR 3 MINUTES WITHOUT STIRRING. REDUCE HEAT TO LOW, ADD MARSHMALLOWS, AND STIR UNTIL THEY ARE COMPLETELY MELTED AND MIXTURE IS SMOOTH, ABOUT 4 MINUTES. REMOVE FROM HEAT AND, USING THE ELECTRIC MIXER ON LOW SPEED, BEAT HOT MARSHMALLOW MIXTURE INTO THE EGG WHITES. CONTINUE BEATING FOR 2 MINUTES. BEAT IN VANILLA. SERVE WARM OR COLD.

SAUCE MAY BE REFRIGERATED IN AN AIRTIGHT CONTAINER FOR UP TO 3 WEEKS. TO RE-HEAT, MICROWAVE ON LOW POWER FOR 30 SECONDS, OR UNTIL WARM. MAKES 3 CUPS.

CLASSIC CARAMEL SYRUP

1 cup granulated sugar	*1 cup heavy cream*
¹/₃ cup water	

COMBINE SUGAR AND WATER IN A HEAVY MEDIUM-SIZE SAUCEPAN. STIR CONSTANTLY OVER MEDIUM HEAT UNTIL SUGAR IS DISSOLVED AND THE MIXTURE COMES TO A BOIL. STOP STIRRING AND BOIL UNTIL THE MIXTURE TURNS A DEEP CARAMEL COLOR (6-12 MINUTES). WATCH CAREFULLY TO MAKE SURE MIXTURE DOESN'T GET TOO DARK.

REMOVE FROM HEAT AND ADD CREAM (CAUTION: MIXTURE WILL BUBBLE UP FIERCELY). RETURN PAN TO HIGH HEAT AND BOIL, STIRRING OCCASIONALLY, FOR 2 MINUTES. REMOVE FROM HEAT AND POUR INTO A GLASS MEASURING CUP OR OTHER HEATPROOF CONTAINER. ALLOW TO COOL TO DESIRED TEMPERATURE.

SYRUP CAN BE REFRIGERATED IN AN AIRTIGHT CONTAINER FOR UP TO 3 WEEKS TO REHEAT, MICROWAVE ON LOW POWER AT 15-SECOND INTERVALS, OR UNTIL WARM. MAKES 1 CUP.

TOP BANANA IN THE BIG APPLE

The cathedral-like vault underneath the Manhattan side of the 59th Street Bridge is home to Guastavino's, where the sheer scale of the restaurant inspires a dazzling Banana Split topped with macadamia nut brittle. Executive Chef Daniel Orr believes a Sundae should have everything you usually allow yourself. In a word, a "birthday" in a dish. Best of all, you can celebrate even if it's not the anniversary of your birth, or it is but you've no intention of revealing your age.

FRIED BANANA SPLIT

1 semi-ripe banana
Tempura batter to cover banana, recipe follows
Vegetable oil
1 ounce chocolate sauce
1 ounce butterscotch sauce
1 ounce marshmallow syrup

1 large scoop each of vanilla, chocolate and strawberry ice cream
Unsweetened whipped cream
Toasted shredded coconut, recipe follows
Macadamia brittle, recipe follows

CUT THE BANANA IN HALF LENGTHWISE AND LIGHTLY DIP INTO THE TEMPURA BATTER. SUBMERGE THE BATTER-COVERED BANANA SLICES IN VEGETABLE OIL TO DEEP-FRY THEM TO BROWN. REMOVE FROM POT AND DRAIN. PLACE THE BANANA HALVES ALONG THE EDGES OF AN OVAL PLATTER, THEN LINE UP ONE LARGE SCOOP OF EACH ICE CREAM IN THE CENTER. LADLE BUTTERSCOTCH SAUCE OVER THE VANILLA ICE CREAM, CHOCOLATE SYRUP OVER THE CHOCOLATE ICE CREAM, AND MARSHMALLOW SYRUP OVER THE STRAWBERRY ICE CREAM. GARNISH WITH WHIPPED CREAM AND TOASTED COCONUT. SPRINKLE WITH MACADAMIA BRITTLE.

- ADAPTED FROM GUASTAVINO'S, NEW YORK, NEW YORK

TEMPURA BATTER
FOR FRIED BANANAS

1 egg	1 cup all-purpose flour
1 cup very cold water	

BEAT EGG IN THE BOWL. ADD WATER TO THE EGG AND MIX WELL. ADD FLOUR AND MIX LIGHTLY. THIS MAKES ENOUGH TO COVER 12 BANANA HALVES (6 BANANAS SLICED LENGTHWISE).

(TO MAKE FRIED TEMPURA BANANA, LIGHTLY DIP BANANA HALVES IN BATTER AND DEEP FRY IN VEGETABLE OIL.)

TOASTED SHREDDED COCONUT
(OR ALMONDS)

This recipe can also be used for toasted almonds, substituting 1 cup of slivered or chopped almonds for the shredded coconut.

SPREAD ONE CUP OF SHREDDED COCONUT ON UNGREASED COOKIE SHEET. TOAST IN A 300-DEGREE OVEN, STIRRING OCCASIONALLY UNTIL COCONUT JUST BEGINS TO TURN A LIGHT GOLDEN COLOR, ABOUT 25 MINUTES. MAKES ENOUGH FOR 6 BANANA SPLITS.

MACADAMIA BRITTLE

10 ounces macadamia nuts	2 ounces butter
1 pound sugar	1/2 teaspoon kosher salt
1 teaspoon lemon juice	

TOAST NUTS ON A SHALLOW PAN IN OVEN UNTIL SLIGHTLY BROWN, APPROXIMATELY 5 MINUTES AT 400 DEGREES. COARSELY CHOP THEM AND SET ASIDE. PLACE SUGAR IN A PAN WITH A HEAVY BOTTOM AND CARAMELIZE TO A LIGHT BROWN COLOR, APPROXIMATELY 8 TO 10 MINUTES OVER A MEDIUM FLAME. REMOVE FROM HEAT QUICKLY AND ADD THE LEMON JUICE TO "BREAK" THE CARAMEL. BE CAREFUL OF THE SIZZLE WHEN YOU DO THIS. THEN STIR IN THE BUTTER AND SALT, AND FOLD IN THE NUTS. POUR ONTO A SHALLOW NON-STICK TRAY AND SMOOTH OUT TO A UNIFORM 2/3-INCH THICKNESS. COOL TO ROOM TEMPERATURE, THEN STORE IN AN AIRTIGHT CONTAINER BETWEEN PIECES OF PARCHMENT PAPER. CRUMBLE AS NEEDED. MAKES ENOUGH FOR A DOZEN BANANA SPLITS OR OTHER SUNDAES.

BANANAS FOSTER

The boozy Louisiana banana split variation, known as Bananas Foster, is one few diners willingly share, even when it's served at brunch. Ella Brennan melded a cooked-banana recipe of her mother's with the banana split concept, and named it after a regular Brennan's customer, Richard Foster. Brennan's, a must New Orleans stop for visitors, uses 35,000 pounds of bananas every year.

• •

¹/₄ cup (¹/₂ stick) butter	4 bananas, cut in half length-
1 cup brown sugar	wise, then halved
¹/₂ teaspoon cinnamon	¹/₄ cup dark rum
¹/₄ cup banana liqueur	4 large scoops vanilla ice cream

• •

COMBINE THE BUTTER, SUGAR, AND CINNAMON IN A FLAMBĒ PAN OR SKILLET. PLACE THE PAN OVER LOW HEAT, EITHER ON AN ALCOHOL BURNER OR ON TOP OF THE STOVE, AND COOK, STIRRING CONSTANTLY UNTIL THE SUGAR DISSOLVES. STIR IN THE BANANA LIQUEUR, THEN PLACE THE BANANAS IN THE PAN. WHEN THE BANANAS SOFTEN AND BEGIN TO BROWN, CAREFULLY ADD THE RUM. CONTINUE TO COOK THE SAUCE UNTIL THE RUM IS HOT, THEN TIP THE PAN SLIGHTLY TO IGNITE THE RUM. WHEN THE FLAMES SUBSIDE, LIFT THE BANANAS OUT OF THE PAN AND PLACE FOUR PIECES EACH OVER PORTIONS OF ICE CREAM IN 4 DISHES. GENEROUSLY SPOON WARM SAUCE OVER THE TOP OF THE ICE CREAM AND SERVE IMMEDIATELY.

- BRENNAN'S, NEW ORLEANS, LOUISIANA

Chapter 6

ROARING SUNDAES

"They stood in front of the jewelry stores and picked out their engagement rings and their wedding rings and their platinum wrist watches, and then drifted off to inspect the feather fans and opera cloaks; meanwhile digesting the sandwiches and Sundaes they had eaten for lunch."

– F. SCOTT FITZGERALD, *MAY DAY*

How ya gonna wet your whistle when the whole darn world goes dry? The Prohibition gong came down in 1920. Legal alcohol was out; ice cream was in. The Sundae became our above-board, national indulgence.

And what a time those twelve years, ten months and nineteen days were! Gangsters, jazz, bobbed hair, flagpole-sitting and a dizzying whirl of ice cream marked the era.

Some taverns went backroom, up a staircase, down into the basement. Many converted into soda fountains. Distillers found new lines. Adolph Coors converted his Golden, Colorado, brewery to a malted-milk plant. In St. Louis, Anheuser-Busch dumped Budweiser for the duration, and became an ice cream factory.

In Chicago, "Hinky Dink" Kenna, well-known saloon keeper and his partner, the cigar-puffing politician "Bathhouse" Coughlin, opened The Ladies and Gents Ice Cream Parlor, a 1,200-seat enterprise.

The Savoy Ballroom in Harlem opened its doors in 1926. "Gangster Moe" Paddon ran the joint as a front for the mob, but Paddon resented the imputation that he was a racketeer and insisted his business was 100 per cent legit. The two-story club spanned the block of 140th Street to 141st Street on Lenox Avenue.

Its immense dance floor was packed nightly by a jostling, bouncing, swaying multitude. The Savoy was a home of swing—there one first saw the dances all America would copy. It's said that while a throng celebrated Charles Lindbergh's 1927 Paris landing, Savoy regular, "Shorty George" Snowden, and his girl improvised new steps. When a reporter interrupted the dancers to ask the name of their dance, George glanced over at a tab headline proclaiming "Lindy Hops the Atlantic," and replied, "the Lindy Hop."

Savoy bartenders supposedly poured only soft drinks, while at its elegant soda fountain spiffy soda jerks served up ice cream floats, banana splits and Sundaes.

More ice cream was commercially produced than ever during the

MENU COVER FROM THE SAVOY.

ICE CREAM ON A STICK

☙

*I*n 1920, Harry Burt, an ice cream parlor operator in Youngstown, Ohio, copied the lollypop and put an ice cream bar on a stick. He took to the streets to sell his new invention from a white truck outfitted with bells. Eventually, he spawned a fleet of "Good Humor" men, each in the pressed and spotless white uniform of a soda jerk, with a white hat, shiny Sam Browne belt and black bow tie.

The Good Humor man was trained to be courteous, raising his cap to women, and providing men with a crisp salute.

Radio funnyman Fred Allen once joked about the cannibal chief with a sweet tooth: "For dessert he always eats a Good Humor Man."

glamorous '20s, and competition became keen enough for the quality of commercial ice cream to go up. The use of sweetened condensed milk—whole milk condensed to half its volume and mixed with pure cane sugar—turned out a smoother, richer product.

History seemed to accelerate to double-time in the decade that roared. Liberation from the conventions that had restricted young people's social lives before World War I meant that chaperones were out and double dating was in. Teenagers watched double features, then enjoyed "double dip" cones or shared "double scoop" Sundaes.

And it wasn't just "flaming youth" who wanted twice as much of everything. The Twin Sundae, a favorite in Minnesota drugstores, was a doubly delectable dessert with two scoops of ice cream side by side, topped with the usual Sundae dressings. It may have started as a date dish, but it soon resonated far beyond duos and in circles distant from Minneapolis and St. Paul.

Bathtub gin and its like, of course, also boomed. But much of the homemade booze—mixed from industrial alcohol, juniper berries and glycerin—was just barely palatable. When it was discovered that the sweetness of chocolate killed the bitterness of synthetic gin, candy bars joined silver flasks in pockets and purses. Several nickel candy brands, including Mounds, Milky Way, Reese's Peanut Butter Cup and Tootsie Roll, were launched during Prohibition. In the swinging ferment of the time, more chocolate and bits of candy bars began showing up in Sundaes.

If there was any doubt about America's ice cream obsession, the 1920s erased it. By 1929, sixty percent of the nation's 58,258 drugstores had installed soda fountains. The modest drugstore soda fountain had become the most popular public gathering place in a dry America. In big cities, there were lavish, upscale, chandeliered ice cream emporiums, some with swing music, which surely can be seen as an embellishment on the Ice Cream Quick-Step. The saloon on all social levels had come back home.

I can't prove that the Sundae was the most-served dish in ice cream parlors, low and high, of that time, although the spurt of Sundae invention during that era suggests it. But, I ask you, what are cocktails after all, in their fancy names with their fruit garnishes? They're alcoholic Sundaes. In my opinion, the day they removed the booze, the ice cream cocktail really took off. The Sundae was already a testament to the American genius for invention and reinvention. And it beautifully matched the roaring '20s temperament in splash, indulgence and wackiness.

THE RECIPES

COLD FUDGE BABY RUTH

DIP ONE LARGE SCOOP OF VANILLA ICE CREAM INTO A SUNDAE TULIP. COVER THE ICE CREAM WITH A LADLEFUL OF COLD FUDGE, GARNISH WITH WHIPPED CREAM, AND PLACE A SLICE OF A BABY RUTH CANDY BAR ON TOP.

– CANDYLAND, GRINNELL, IOWA

SPOTTED DOG SUNDAE

This Sundae not only has a great name, it typifies the double-the-fun spirit of the '20s.

LADLE 2 OUNCES OF CHOCOLATE SYRUP INTO THE BOTTOM OF A TALL SUNDAE GOBLET. ADD ONE LARGE SCOOP OF CHOCOLATE ICE CREAM, THEN ONE LARGE SCOOP OF VANILLA ICE CREAM, AND COVER WITH ANOTHER 2 OUNCES OF CHOCOLATE SYRUP. GARNISH WITH WHIPPED CREAM, AND PLACE A MARASCHINO CHERRY AT THE TOP.

− DINTY MOORE'S, BOSTON, MASSACHUSSETTS

LUCKY LINDY SUNDAE

DIP ONE LARGE SCOOP OF CHOCOLATE ICE CREAM INTO A TALL SUNDAE GOBLET, AND COVER ICE CREAM WITH 2 CRUSHED MACAROONS, 2 OUNCES OF CHOCOLATE SYRUP AND A PINCH OF SHREDDED COCONUT. THEN ADD ONE LARGE SCOOP OF VANILLA ICE CREAM, GARNISH WITH WHIPPED CREAM AND PLACE A MARASCHINO CHERRY AT THE TOP.

− SAVOY BALLROOM, NEW YORK, NEW YORK

BEE'S KNEES

Hollywood flapper Mabel Normand was a Sundae inspiration. Not only did the silent film comedienne dress in the loose, saucy, short dresses that signified freedom, she flaunted her independence in all aspects of style. When she confessed that she poured honey over ice cream every day for breakfast, soda jerks responded with a loving tribute.

INTO A SUNDAE TULIP POUR $\frac{1}{2}$ OUNCE OF PURE HONEY, THEN ADD ONE LARGE SCOOP OF VANILLA ICE CREAM. POUR AN ADDITIONAL OUNCE OF HONEY OVER THE ICE CREAM, SPRINKLE WITH ROASTED, SALTED ALMONDS. TOP WITH WHIPPED CREAM AND A MARASCHINO.

− STEVENS ICE CREAM, LOS ANGELES, CALIFORNIA

PINK LADY

Give whipped cream a pink tint by adding a small amount of strawberry juice. Set aside.

Pour ½ ounce of pineapple syrup into the bottom of a Sundae tulip, then add one large scoop of vanilla ice cream. Top with the pink whipped cream. Sprinkle on chocolate-dipped peanuts and place a maraschino at the top.

– Blue Bird Restaurant and Soda Grill, Elyria, Ohio

MANHATTAN SUNDAE

Dip one small scoop of vanilla ice cream into a champagne coupe. Cover with champagne syrup (a "simple syrup" made with 1 part champagne to 2 parts sugar, stirred till the sugar dissolves), garnish with whipped cream and place a whole strawberry on the top.

– Gutman's, New York, New York

Chapter 7

SUNDAE RULES

❧

*"We got the hot fudge on the bottom . . . that allows
you to control the fudge distribution while you're
eating your ice cream."*

– Jerry Seinfeld

Ho Jo began not because citizens were forced to give up boozy cocktails, but because guys gave up cigars and joined the dolls in cigarettes. This left the wholesale cigar business Howard Deering Johnson had inherited from his father in such deep debt that he was forced to close it. When the smoke cleared, Johnson, 28, sold his yellow Stutz Bearcat and put it toward the purchase of a small corner drugstore in his hometown of Wollaston, on the coast of Massachusetts. It was 1925, and "Buster," as he was called in the family, reckoned that if ice cream was so popular, then better-tasting ice cream would be even

A PRISTINE HO JO FOUNTAIN BEFORE THE OPENING BELL.

more popular and his marble-topped soda fountain would prosper.

Buster Johnson started with "secret formula" vanilla and chocolate. The secret was that his ice creams, made of all natural ingredients, contained twice the butterfat (the cream content of milk) of other brands. Despite the super-premium ice creams in his Sundaes, he initially kept them at the going ten-cent price. Customers flooded his fountain. And when summer came, Johnson added a beachfront stand that sold $60,000 worth of ice cream cones, at a nickel apiece, its first season.

Between his stand and his soda fountain he did a quarter of a million dollars worth of ice cream business in 1928, and went on to open his first restaurant in Quincy, Massachusetts, on the ground floor of a ten-story granite "skyscraper." The menu had all the later-famous Howard Johnson dishes—fried clams, baked beans and Sundaes. And like all subsequent Ho Jo eateries, it offered a dazzling twenty-eight ice cream flavors. "I thought I had every flavor in the world," he would later say.

Quincy, home of the first father-and-son presidents, John and John Quincy Adams, was a Yankee-hearted town, and Buster Johnson kept up its theme in his restaurant's decor, which featured knotty pine paneling and ruffled curtains.

Johnson planned to add restaurants almost immediately, but his plans were squelched when the '20s roar was choked into a squeak on October 24, 1929. Johnson's bank-loan officer ended up working as a caddy at his old country club. But in 1935, Buster persuaded former schoolmate Reginald Sprague to open up a restaurant bearing the Howard Johnson name in Orleans on Cape Cod. The deal Johnson worked out with Sprague effectively invented a new American business form: the franchise. By the following summer, there were fifteen more Howard Johnson restaurants. The deal was the same—it was Howard Johnson's way or the highway—and the formula was a success.

Roofs of Howard Johnson's roadside shrines were sheathed in porcelain tiles, painted bright orange because Johnson had been assured by a Boston University professor that orange reflected light; a Howard Johnson's would be visible from far enough away so a car could slow down and enter its parking lot. Cupolas and weathervanes sustained the remnant Yankee decorative flavor: waitresses wore starched blue and orange dresses.

Each restaurant adhered to what company men and women colloquially called "Howard Johnson bible" standards for everything, including Sundaes, which were made with a special #16 Conical Scoop.

(It's unlikely that even Seinfeld could have gotten a Sundae his way—with the fudge on the bottom—if a classically trained Ho-Jo scooper was on the job.) Here are the bible's Sundae rules.

A. *Shake scoop to remove excess water.*
B. *Hold the scoop firmly, with your thumb under the release. The closer your hand is to the head of the scoop, the better leverage you have. This lessens the strain on your wrist.*
C. *With the scoop FACING YOU, dip into the ice cream approximately 1/4 inch. DO NOT face the scoop downward and attempt to dig a hole.*
D. *Draw the scoop toward you, along the edge of the container, in a clockwise motion. The ice cream is forced into one side of the scoop and out the opposite side, forming a "lip."*
E. *When the portions have been removed, the container should appear with the ice cream higher in the middle than at the sides.*

"The history of the Howard Johnson's restaurants is my own history," its founder once proclaimed. "Their beginning was mine; their reputation was mine to preserve." A portrait of Buster once hung in every establishment, looking down to see that every Sundae was scooped just right.

In the late 1970s, there were over 1,000 Ho Jo restaurants. Today, there are only seventeen franchises left.

THE RECIPES

CLASSIC BUTTERSCOTCH SAUCE

1 1/2 cups packed dark brown sugar	1 1/2 cups heavy cream
3/4 cup water	1 teaspoon pure vanilla extract

STIR BROWN SUGAR AND WATER TOGETHER IN A LARGE, HEAVY SAUCEPAN. BRING TO A BOIL OVER HIGH HEAT. REDUCE HEAT TO MEDIUM AND COOK FOR 2 TO 3 MINUTES AT A FULL BOIL, STIRRING OCCASIONALLY, UNTIL IT HAS THICKENED SLIGHTLY. REMOVE FROM HEAT.

Whisk in cream and then return to a boil, whisking constantly. Once the mixture is boiling, whisk only occasionally and cook for 5 minutes over high heat, lowering heat slightly if the sauce bubbles too high and threatens to boil over. Remove from heat and whisk in vanilla. Allow to cool slightly (mixture will be very hot). Serve warm.

Sauce can be refrigerated in an airtight container for up to 3 weeks. To reheat, microwave at 15-second intervals until warm. Makes 2 cups.

HO JO TRIUMPHS

ICECAPADE

Dip three small scoops of fruit sherbet (customer chooses the flavors) into a wide Sundae dish to form a triangle. Add one small scoop vanilla ice cream on top. Ladle 2 ounces of sliced strawberries and 2 ounces of crushed pineapple over the ice cream. Decorate with whipped cream and place a maraschino on the top.

SCOTCH AND FUDGE

Place one large scoop of peppermint candy-stick ice cream and one large scoop of vanilla ice cream side by side in a wide Sundae dish. Ladle 2 ounces of hot fudge sauce over the peppermint ice cream, and 2 ounces of hot butterscotch sauce over the vanilla. Layer with whipped cream and don't forget the cherry on top.

DIXIE SNOWBALL

Roll one large, round scoop of vanilla ice cream in fresh, shredded coconut, then place coconut-covered ice cream ball in a Sundae tulip. Ladle on 2 ounces of hot fudge sauce and sprinkle with shredded, toasted coconut.

Chapter 8

FOUNTAIN SPEAK

"You scream, I scream,
They all scream for ice cream.
Tuesdays, Mondays,
They all scream for Sundaes."

– University of Kansas cheer, 1920s

"Drop a bucket of mud with a black bottom!"
Translation: Dish up a Hot Fudge Sundae with chocolate ice cream.

What you just heard was a waiter barking an order to a soda jerk at the old Jayhawk Café in Lawrence, Kansas, but it could have been practically any ice cream fountain during the glory days of the 20s and 30s.

Sadly, the great American dialect of Fountain Speak has all but disappeared. Fewer and fewer Americans recall the cheerful (or sometimes harried) demand for "a crowd of houseboats" which used to be the way an order for three banana splits was registered. Three's a crowd, you know. And houseboat is shorter and sassier than "banana boat," which itself is shorthand for the glassware in which a banana split typically is served.

Once upon a time, one didn't need a Palm Pilot in the college town of Lawrence. If you hoped to run into a friend, all you needed was to sit in the Jayhawk and wait for everyone you knew to stop in.

"Professor" Paul Sinclair started as a waiter at this finishing school for soda jerks; eventually he purchased the place. Although this professor of Ice Cream retired and closed the Jayhawk's doors in 1964, his lively, sweet phrases remain of academic interest to Michael Owen Jones, professor of history and folklore at UCLA.

No one loved Fountain Speak more than Sinclair, explains Jones, and Sinclair made sure the code was passed down to generations of apostles. Sinclair realized that its colorful goofiness entertained alert soda-fountain customers, but mainly he treasured its efficiency. Fountain Speak not only abbreviated orders in the bustling Jayhawk, it was a terrific memory aid. It's human nature to remember things that are amusing, and so many of the "calls"—as the entire description of the dish being ordered was known—were hoots.

The origin and evolution of many words and phrases have been lost. Take "Chicago," for example. Chicago wasn't just a city in Illinois. It was the Jayhawk term for pineapple. How the name of a northern city became the tag for a tropical fruit is a mystery. But Chicago Sundaes were made with pineapples in Lawrence.

Fountain Speak terms varied region to region, sometimes from drugstore to drugstore in the same area. "Black and white" meant "coffee with cream" in some places, a Sundae with vanilla ice cream and chocolate syrup in others; while elsewhere "black and white" referred strictly to a particular ice cream soda.

Calls not only described menu items, they included the number of items in the order, the size of an item and special instructions.

"Burn a crowd of van" relayed an order for three vanilla malteds, "burn" being Fountain Speak for malted.

A call of "ninety-five" sounded the alarm when a customer was skip-

WHAT ELSE IS IN A NAME?

The centerpiece of the soda fountain was a tap from which mineral water (the first soda) was drawn. The moniker "soda jerk" came from the jerking motions required to draw carbonated water from the pumps and levers behind the counter.

The soda jerk was also known as the "fizzician," an expert at adding fizz to a soda or syrup to a Sundae. A good fizzician knew exactly how much topping to ladle on: if too little was added, the syrup would be gone before the ice cream; too much and a puddle remained after the ice cream was gone. A well-trained soda jerk never let syrups run over the edge of the Sundae glass and never ever gave out spoons with sticky handles.

THE RED EXCLAMATION POINT!

he name maraschino derives from the Italian word, "marasca", which is what Italians called the liquor distilled from the bitter, wild Dalmatian cherry. Early maraschinos were cultivated cherries that had been steeped in "marasca." But traditional maraschinos yielded in the marketplace to the seemingly healthier, non-alcoholic cherries bathed in Red Dye No. 2, which were easier to manufacture and invariably neon red. We know today that was a big mistake. Commercial cherries are still called maraschinos, but the fiery color is now the result of a synthetic dye, known both as FD&C Red No. 40 or Allura Red. To keep the fruit longer, it is candy-coated in a fructose slur, a heated sugar mixture that dries and condenses as it cools.

ping out on the bill; "ninety-nine" referred to the head soda jerk at Jayhawk and "ninety-eight" to the assistant. "Psst ninety-eight," meant the assistant manager was snooping.

"Eighty-seven and a half," announced there was a looker out front, which seems more obscure than the term the male screwballs behind the counter used to direct each other's attention to a coed in a tight sweater: "Fix the pumps."

Sundaes or "college ices" boasted a Jayhawk vocabulary of their own, since they were the more frequently ordered treats. "Drop" was the synonym for a scoop of ice cream and each flavor drop had a name of its own. "Mud" was chocolate and "patch" was strawberry. "Globs" covered the drops; many "tulips"named after the shape of the Sundae glass—also required "rocks," meaning nuts.

Although Fountain Speak is no longer a robust dialect in Lawrence, today's K.U. students love ice cream. Sundae Socials mark campus social life, and Lawrence boasts an ice cream parlor across from the old Varsity Theater, which serves edible Sundae dishes, made in an old-fashioned waffle iron and then molded in bowl shape over an old malt cup. The parlor is called Sylas and Maddy's, signifying not a new direction in ice cream talk, but the names of its owners' pets—a red tabby (Sylas) and a terrier mix (Maddy).

SPRINKLE PLENTY

"Jimmies" is an old fountain term for chocolate sprinkles, but these chocolate-candy slivers have as many other names as a good shake of the stuff—including sparkles, decorettes, shots, spirals (even when not so shaped), candy ants and chocolate-covered ants. And I'll eat my Sundae un-jimmied if readers of this book don't inform me of more.

Moreover, some Sundae linguists say that "jimmies" also refer to rainbow sprinkles; others insist such an extension of meaning goes beyond any fair call.

THE RECIPES

CLASSIC
HOT FUDGE SAUCE

The chocolate really must be in small bits or flakes to melt evenly. And a candy thermometer will help you get your sauce perfect.

8 ounces unsweetened chocolate, grated or cut up fine
1/4 cup sweet butter
1 cup sugar

1 cup water
Pinch of salt
3 tablespoons light corn syrup
1/4 cup heavy cream

MELT CHOCOLATE AND BUTTER IN MICROWAVE OR IN A DOUBLE BOILER SET
OVER HOT, SIMMERING WATER. IN A MEDIUM-SIZE HEAVY SAUCEPAN COMBINE
SUGAR, WATER, CORN SYRUP AND SALT AND COOK OVER MEDIUM HEAT, STIRRING
FREQUENTLY, UNTIL THE SUGAR DISSOLVES, ABOUT 5 MINUTES. STOP STIRRING,
BUT CONTINUE COOKING UNTIL MIXTURE REACHES 234 DEGREES ON A CANDY
THERMOMETER, ABOUT 10-15 MINUTES. REMOVE FROM HEAT AND STIR THIS
SYRUP INTO THE CHOCOLATE AND BUTTER MIXTURE. WHISK IN THE CREAM.

IF NOT USING RIGHT AWAY, THE SAUCE MAY BE REFRIGERATED IN AN AIR-
TIGHT CONTAINER AND KEPT FOR A MONTH. REHEAT OVER A DOUBLE BOILER,
WHISKING VIGOROUSLY. IF RE-HEATING OVER DIRECT HEAT, USE VERY LOW
FLAME, AND BE CAREFUL NOT TO LET THE SAUCE BUBBLE OR BURN. MAKES 2 CUPS.

A CROWD OF JAYHAWK SUNDAES

CHICAGO

DIP ONE LARGE SCOOP OF VANILLA ICE CREAM INTO A TULIP. COVER WITH A LADLEFUL OF CRUSHED PINEAPPLE, THEN WHIPPED CREAM; PLACE A CHERRY ON TOP.

DUSTY MILLER

One Fountain Speak legacy is that a "dusty" Sundae continues to mean one brushed or sprinkled with malt powder. If there was indeed someone named Dusty Miller behind this creation, he or she remains a mystery.

DIP ONE LARGE SCOOP OF VANILLA ICE CREAM INTO A SUNDAE TULIP. DROWN THE "DROP" (SCOOP) IN "MUD" (CHOCOLATE SYRUP) AND GARNISH WITH WHIPPED CREAM. DUST THE WHIPPED CREAM WITH A ROUNDED TEASPOON OF MALTED-MILK POWDER AND PLACE A MARASCHINO CHERRY AT THE TOP.

TOUCHDOWN

In this Sundae, the large Brazil nut represents the football and the diner scores when he reaches the bottom of the dish.

PLACE A CHOCOLATE-COVERED BRAZIL NUT INTO A SUNDAE TULIP, FOLLOWED BY A LARGE DROP (SCOOP) OF BUTTER-PECAN ICE CREAM. TOP THE DROP WITH A LADLEFUL OF HEAVY COFFEE SYRUP, GARNISH WITH WHIPPED CREAM AND A MARASCHINO.

HOT FUDGE WAFFLE DISH SUNDAE

DIP 2 LARGE SCOOPS OF VANILLA BEAN ICE CREAM INTO A WAFFLE DISH. CUT ONE BANANA INTO SLICES AND PLACE AROUND THE ICE CREAM, THEN LADLE 2 OUNCES OF HOT FUDGE SAUCE TO COVER. GARNISH WITH WHIPPED CREAM, SPRINKLE ON SLICED TOASTED ALMONDS, AND PLACE A MARASCHINO CHERRY AT THE TOP.

– SYLAS AND MADDY'S, LAWRENCE, KANSAS

Chapter 9

KEEPING SPIRITS UP

"When the Woolworth's Hot-Fudge-Sundae switch goes on, then I know I really have something."

– ANDY WARHOL

After the 1929 market crash, there weren't many pleasures that average folks could afford, and this gave the dime Sundae a new status. It became a treat for special occasions. At the same time, it possibly became a more frequent indulgence for those who still had a bit of jingle in their pockets. So it was that the Sundae might have become even a greater equalizer.

Sundae vendors, ingenious as ever, modeled new varieties of Sundaes on the happier news of the Depression era.

It may be difficult now to understand how a good-news event, such as the birth and survival of five identical girls—the Dionne quintuplets in Ontario—so completely captured American hearts. Not only did their births seem a miracle in those pre-high-tech days, their childhoods were presented as adorable and charmed. Although we know now that the sisters were used cruelly by both their parents and the government, back then their lives seemed as delicious as, well, a Sundae, and their celebrity was ubiquitous. In the 1935 Marx Brothers movie, *A Night at the Opera*, the characters played by Groucho and Chico negotiate a contract with the memorable clause: "The party of the first part shall be known in this contract as the party of the first part."

"It's a duplicate," explains Groucho at one point. "You know what duplicates are."

"Duplicates," replies Chico. "That's five kids up in Canada."

Could a Sundae be far behind? Several Sundaes were probably ahead of the Marx Brothers routine. (Groucho and his brothers, by the way, had earned their Sundae-eating stripes at the still legendary Richmond Hill, Queens, ice cream parlor, Jahn's.)

Of course, one difficulty with headline Sundaes is that their

THE FUTURE WAS OURS TO SEE

🍒

The 1939 World's Fair in New York City optimistically previewed modernisms that would mark the second half of the 20th century. Dairy stands sold dishes of ice cream for forty cents and Ice Cream Sundaes at fifty. Tourist prices, it would seem—in 1940, a Ford coupe cost only $600. Or, you can just say those Sundae makers were true futurists.

currency may not last. Alf Landon campaigners used a yellow and brown sunflower as a symbol for their candidate in his 1936 race against President Franklin Delano Roosevelt. Although Landon certainly lacked FDR's oratorical gifts—with some measure of understatement, Alf said, "Wherever I have gone in this country I have found Americans"—the Republican had his supporters, not least among them the Chicago entrepreneur who concocted the Sunflower Sundae.

More enduring were the Sundaes served at the nation's biggest five-and-dime chain, Woolworth's. Frank Woolworth had opened his first store in 1879 in thrifty Lancaster, Pennsylvania. By 1913, with a thousand stores nationwide, the company was headquartered in what was then the world's tallest building, the Woolworth Building in Manhattan. The Depression was kinder to Woolworth stores, almost all with lunch counters, than it was to upscale department stores—for obvious reasons. The Sundae remained *the* treat of the lunch counter for decades following the Depression.

In the 1930s, many businesspeople came to Woolworth's for lunch on days they didn't brown-bag it. It's not farfetched to imagine a hungry, budget-watching office clerk ordering a Sundae instead of a sandwich.

Although Woolworth's catered to a broad public in its heyday, even in the darkest economic era there were a few people so rich they didn't need to put aside their pennies for a Sundae.

Yet if there was one big expenditure that glamorous and wealthy celebrities believed was worthwhile, it was the home ice cream fountain. "I wouldn't change places with Susie Glutz who works in an office for anything," said Ginger Rogers, who, in 1930 at the age of 19, was one of the highest-paid working girls in America. The $1,500 she earned weekly enabled her to build a soda fountain in her house.

Another Hollywood kid-at-heart, Walt Disney, had his basement modeled into an ice cream parlor, complete with soda fountain, to entertain his friends with Sundae parties.

Two teenaged brothers, Curtis and Priestly Blake, would have liked nothing better than to treat all their pals to Sundaes, but they had to

COURTESY OF PENNSYLVANIA ACADEMY OF FINE ARTS.

THE SODA FOUNTAIN BY WILLIAM GLACKENS, 1935.

make a living first. They figured they could do that selling ice cream, even in hard times. They were right. They opened their first simple Friendly restaurant in 1936 in Springfield, Massachusetts. They chose the name for the outlook they wanted their business to project. The Friendly spirit worked, and so did their creations. The four-scoop Jim Dandy banana split, first offered in 1939, was a crowd-pleaser for decades.

In 1979, the brothers sold their chain to Hershey. Today's Friendly split has retreated to the basic ice cream flavor trio—vanilla, chocolate and strawberry—but gained a regal banner: Royal Banana Split.

THE RECIPES

DIONNE SURPRISE

DROP 5 SCOOPS OF VANILLA ICE CREAM IN A ROW INTO A BANANA BOAT. GARNISH EACH SCOOP WITH A DOLLOP OF WHIPPED CREAM AND A MARASCHINO CHERRY. ARRANGE A LADLEFUL OF CRUSHED PINEAPPLE ALONG ONE SIDE OF THE DISH AND A LADLEFUL OF CRUSHED STRAWBERRIES ALONG THE OPPOSITE SIDE OF THE DISH.

– PUBLIX DRUGSTORE, SOUTH RIVER, NEW JERSEY

SUNFLOWER SUNDAE

TAKE A RATHER LARGE FLAT DISH, LIKE A DINNER PLATE. LADLE A ROUND DOLLOP OF HOT FUDGE SAUCE IN THE CENTER, WITH BANANA SLICES RADIATING OUTWARD TO FORM THE PETALS. PLACE SCOOPS OF CHOCOLATE ICE CREAM AROUND THE EDGE OF THE DISH. WHEN MADE IN THIS MANNER, THE SUNDAE WILL RESEMBLE THE FORM AND COLORING OF A SUNFLOWER.

– ALF LANDON FOR PRESIDENT COMMITTEE

FREE LUNCH SUNDAE

There really was a free lunch. After the repeal of prohibition, many saloons offered a bar-top array of pickles, hard-boiled eggs and sandwiches without charge to drinkers. But some barkeeps had to repel indigents who raided their food. The booting out of freeloaders became known as the "bum's rush." Free lunch inspired the name of an Ice Cream Sundae.

DROP TWO LARGE SCOOPS OF VANILLA ICE CREAM SIDE BY SIDE INTO A LARGE SUNDAE BOWL. COVER ONE SCOOP WITH CHOCOLATE SYRUP AND A TEASPOON OF MALTED MILK POWDER; COVER THE OTHER SCOOP WITH CARAMEL SYRUP AND A TEASPOON OF CHOPPED PECANS. AT THE TOP OF EACH SCOOP, PLACE A MARASCHINO CHERRY WITH A TOOTHPICK THROUGH IT.

– BRASS RAIL, NEW YORK, NEW YORK

BUDGET SUNDAE

DIP ONE LARGE SCOOP OF VANILLA ICE CREAM INTO A SUNDAE TULIP. ADD CRUSHED FRUIT OR OTHER TOPPING (CHOICE OF STRAWBERRY, PINEAPPLE, CHERRY, CHOCOLATE OR HOT FUDGE). GARNISH WITH WHIPPED CREAM, SPRINKLE WITH ROASTED NUTS, AND FINISH WITH A CHERRY ON THE TOP.

– WOOLWORTH'S

Chapter 10

SUNDAE MAKERS TO THE STARS

"What really distinguishes ice cream parlors is their atmosphere, and therein lies the difference between a Sundae that satisfies the palate and one that satisfies the soul."

– Fran R. Schumer

Some like it hot . . . fudge. And others don't care what the flavor is when they spot a girl with porcelain skin and high cheekbones, wearing a sweater two sizes too small, eating an ice cream treat. That girl was Lana Turner, and the story has it that she was eating it in Schwab's, one of Hollywood's two late and lamented Sundae greats.

Tinseltown lies somewhere between reality and dream, and memory has a way of both twisting and oversimplifying the past, but the legend goes like this: A 17-year-old looker named Judy Turner skipped her typing class at Hollywood High School one day in 1937 and ducked into nearby Schwab's Pharmacy to satisfy a sweet tooth. Billy Wilkerson, publisher of *Hollywood Reporter*, spotted her at the marble-topped soda fountain bar, eased onto the adjoining stool and purred, "Every pretty young girl wants to be in the movies, and I think you'd be perfect."

In her 1982 autobiography, Turner remembered it thus: "He didn't seem to want to pick me up, because he didn't make idle chatter."

But she said the encounter had been in the Top Hat Cafe down the street, not Schwab's. Credit is everything, as every Hollywood denizen knows. Schwab's had received the credit so long ago that no correction could stick.

Wilkerson introduced Judy to a talent agent, who introduced her to director Mervyn LeRoy, who was looking for a girl with that elusive combination of sex appeal and innocence. Two months later, "Lana Turner" was eating ice cream with Mickey Rooney, Judy Garland

and Ann Rutherford between takes on the motion picture, *Love Finds Andy Hardy*. Lana Turner's life turned out not to be a bowl of maraschinos but, oh, what a sweet beginning.

Schwab's was in the orbit of the stars before Turner's name became forever linked with it. In 1932, the four Schwab brothers—Jack, Leon, Bernard and Marvin—had abandoned their first L.A. outpost to re-establish their drug and food counters at Sunset Boulevard and Crescent Heights. Refugees from the night before stumbled in, seeking hangover cures. Early risers like George Burns made it a breakfast stop. Agents and managers dropped by to use the phone booths.

But it was in 1933, when *Photoplay* gossip columnist Sidney Skolsky rented an apartment two doors down from the store, that Schwab's became famous. Skolsky nicknamed the drugstore "the Schwabedero," as he chronicled the comings and goings of such patrons as Errol Flynn and Rita Hayworth. Regulars also included John Barrymore, Orson Welles, Ava Gardner and Tallulah Bankhead. Charlie Chaplin played pinball in the back room.

Judy Garland, who quipped she was born at the age of twelve on an MGM lot, also said she had her first real date at fifteen when Johnny Downs took her to an evening movie, then to Schwab's for a chocolate Sundae with whipped cream, nuts and a cherry. On that occasion, she remembered, she wore a navy blue gingham dress with blue bobby sox and flat-heeled shoes. And songwriter Harold Arlen wrote "Over the Rainbow" in a corner booth, perhaps inspired by the glimmer of Schwab's neon sign. Years later, but not as many years later as it should

---

NOW THAT'S ENTERTAINMENT!

🍒

"*Asking me what I think of Oscar [Hammerstein] is like asking me what I think of the Yankees, Man o' War and strawberry Sundaes.*" –BILLY ROSE

"*In all my films, all the great things are put together. It's not like one kind of ice cream but rather a very big Sundae.*" –GEORGE LUCAS

have been, a Schwab's delivery boy dropped off a single sleeping pill at Judy Garland's house each evening.

James Dean, Telly Savalas and Jack Nicholson included Schwab's on their rounds. And a 21-year-old Elvis Presley brought Natalie Wood there on a date. "Elvis was so square, we went out for Hot Fudge Sundaes at Schwab's," she would later tell an interviewer. "He didn't drink, he didn't swear, he didn't even smoke, it was like having the date that I never had in high school." She added, "He didn't take [his talent] for granted. Elvis had to be nice to people, otherwise God would take it all away."

New York writers under studio contract, such as John O'Hara and Dorothy Parker, met at Schwab's to kibitz about life back East. On occasion, Parker was joined by Robert Benchley, who lived in a Garden of Allah villa, directly across Sunset. Benchley was so terrified of traffic that he called taxis to ferry him across the street.

Billy Wilder's classic 1950 movie, *Sunset Boulevard*, featured a re-created interior of Schwab's. Its protagonist, Joe Gillis (William Holden) says in a voice-over, "I drove down to headquarters. That's the way a lot of us think about Schwab's. Kind of a combination office, *kaffee klatsch* and waiting room."

Schwab's, which closed its doors in 1986, was not the only Sundae maker to the stars—or to the wannabes. Until C.C. Brown's owners scooped their last Sundae in 1996, that extravaganza of an ice cream parlor ranked high among the cognoscenti. And it had one of the all-time Hollywood long runs.

Sundae-dreaming Clarence Clifton Brown opened his Los Angeles ice cream and candy shop in 1906. Hair parted debonairly down the middle, he resembled a banker more than a candy maker, a lawyer more than a soda jerk. Yet, for years he labored every day in the kitchen at the back of his store, making candies and ice cream to sell up front. The confection that obsessed him was hot fudge sauce.

Stardust floats off, but a great hot fudge sauce recipe is forever. The making of his liquid fudge depended on subtleties and complexities in the blending of the sugars, as well as the high boiling temperatures in his copper kettle. Clarence Brown patiently reworked his hot fudge formula for twenty years until it was perfect every time.

Emboldened by his success, in 1929 he moved the business to Hollywood Boulevard, a few doors down from Grauman's Chinese Theatre. Ah, Hollywood! It's hard to imagine a location more suited to merchandising the epic Sundae than the neighborhood where our

larger-than-life heroes and heroines leave their small footprints outside of what's now known as Mann's Chinese Theater.

C.C. Brown's was designed in larger-than-life proportions, with glass double doors, huge candy display cases, a theatrical 30-foot-high ceiling, and a cinematic black and white interior. The perpetual motion inside could very well have taken place on a studio set: non-stop ice cream dipping, frantic servers navigating the narrow aisles of tables with trays of Sundaes, and cash register bells ringing incessantly.

Hollywood celebrities instantly felt at home there. The likes of Mary Pickford, Joan Crawford, Barbara Stanwyck, Jack Benny, Jackie Cooper and Jack Lemmon all were part of Brown's cast of Sundae eaters. The famous ice cream parlor granted the flashbulb-shy a measure of privacy in its high-back black walnut booths around the perimeter of the establishment. But this was not enough protection for Marlon Brando, who'd roll up to C.C. Brown in his limo. Brando, ensconced in the parked car, would gobble his Sundae privately while his family ate inside.

The best-selling Hot Fudge Sundae was listed on the menu as "The Last Act," since it was a moviegoer tradition to stop in for the famous dessert after theater house lights went back on. C.C. Brown

C.C. BROWN'S OF HOLLYWOOD AT NIGHT.

knew how to make the star struck happy even when no screen gods or goddesses could be glimpsed.

With a flourish, a server delivered silver goblets piled with good vanilla ice cream, genuine whipped cream and chopped, roasted almonds. Small brown ceramic pitchers of hot fudge, resting in a hot-water bath, accompanied the goblets, allowing you to pour the fudge over the top of the ice cream in one fell swoop or parcel it out over the course of eating your Sundae. If you used just a little at a time, the fudge sauce kept warmer, and there always seemed to be enough to insure that you wouldn't run out.

Clarence Clifton Brown left the business to his son, who hired dairy chemist John A. Schumacher. Schumacher, who had been with the Carnation Company and always dressed in white, purchased the emporium in 1958. And Schumacher had the sense to maintain the stellar Sundae performance, remaining true to high-butterfat ice cream, hand-whipped cream and the sensational made-on-the-premises hot fudge sauce. He left the secrets of Clarence Brown's hot fudge to his sons, Tim and John, who continue to make C.C. Brown's Hot Fudge Topping in Calabasas, California, which they market by mail order and through their website.

The connection between Hollywood and Sundaes seems nearly pre-ordained because the spiritual essence of both is youth. Judy Turner was actually still a child when her Sundae habit and the promise of stardom met up, but what I'm really talking about here is that no matter what our age, most of us feel young when we tuck our spoons into a Sundae. For a while, we are the ones whose futures are unwritten; we are as eternally youthful as are the biggest stars whose beauty and youth have forever been captured on celluloid.

Perhaps it was just happenstance that C.C. Brown concocted a great hot fudge sauce in the city of our collective dreams. But maybe, in that dawn of the motion-picture era, there was something in the air that inspired him to keep trying until his topping was as chocolate-y and velvety as his hopes. Certainly, once Brown got the sauce right, he had the best publicity machine in the world working for it.

Whatever—as today's expression goes—the invention of hot fudge sauce was a hard act to follow. But the Oscar for Supporting Actress in a Topping Role would rightly go to Sarah Dow, proprietress of Bailey's Ice Cream Parlor in Boston in the early decades of the 20th century. Dow, it is said, cooked up an angelic hot fudge sauce of her own for the Sundaes that won the hearts of both bluestockings and workers.

Bailey's is gone, too, but forty miles from Hollywood is a soda fountain redolent of the era of Schwab's. Key 1950s scenes for the movie, *That Thing You Do*, starring Tom Hanks, were shot at Watson's Drugs, a fixture in Orange, California, for a century. Since the look of Watson's Drugs had not actually stood still, Hollywood set designers "restored" its soda fountain to the glory days of Sundaes before on-location filming began. Afterwards, the drugstore kept its new "old" Hollywood fountain.

THE RECIPES

THREE STAR POWER SUNDAES

*I*ce cream doused with coffee, as in the "Don't Care Sundae," was a Schwab's stay-awake prescription for people who had been on the set since dawn. The "Pink and Pretty" and "Movie" Sundaes depended on strawberries for their glow.

DON'T CARE SUNDAE

*D*ip one large scoop of vanilla ice cream into a Sundae tulip. Cover the ice cream with coffee syrup and garnish with whipped cream. Sprinkle on chopped nuts and place a maraschino cherry on the top.

COFFEE SYRUP

2 cups strong, brewed coffee   *1/2 teaspoon vanilla extract*
1 cup sugar

*For strong coffee, make three small pots of coffee with the same liquid. Brew the first pot in the usual way. For the second pot, use the first batch of brewed coffee as the liquid instead of water, with fresh coffee grounds; then repeat with twice-brewed coffee and new grounds to produce the final pot.

To make the syrup, heat the thrice-brewed coffee in a saucepan to a simmer. Stir in sugar and vanilla and continue to simmer for 10 minutes, stirring until sugar completely dissolves. Cool before using.

PINK AND PRETTY SUNDAE

DIP ONE LARGE SCOOP OF STRAWBERRY ICE CREAM INTO A SUNDAE TULIP, COVER WITH MARSHMALLOW SYRUP, THEN FINISH WITH STRAWBERRY TOPPING. GARNISH WITH WHIPPED CREAM, AND PLACE A MARASCHINO CHERRY ON THE TOP.

MOVIE SUNDAE

PLACE A HEAPING SPOONFUL OF STRAWBERRY PRESERVE AT THE BOTTOM OF A LONG-STEMMED SUNDAE GOBLET. ADD 2 LARGE SCOOPS OF VANILLA ICE CREAM, SPRINKLE WITH CHOPPED MIXED NUTS AND PLACE TWO LARGE, FRESH STRAWBERRIES AT THE CENTER. SPRINKLE FINELY SHREDDED COCONUT OVER THE TOP.

– SCHWAB'S, LOS ANGELES, CALIFORNIA

FABULOUS FUDGE SUNDAES

Star power isn't completely in the warm chocolate topping—superior ice cream and whipped cream matter, too, yet the quality and quantity of the fudge sauce is of colossal importance.

BUSTER BROWN SUNDAE

PLACE ONE PEELED, FRESH BANANA SLICED IN HALF LENGTHWISE ON A FLAT SUNDAE DISH. ARRANGE ONE LARGE SCOOP OF VANILLA AND ONE LARGE SCOOP OF CHOCOLATE ICE CREAM ON EITHER SIDE. SPRINKLE ON A LAYER OF CHOPPED ROASTED ALMONDS AND GARNISH WITH WHIPPED CREAM. SERVE WITH A PITCHER OF HEATED FUDGE SAUCE.

CHOCOLATE DROP

PLACE ONE PEELED, FRESH BANANA SLICED IN HALF LENGTHWISE ON A FLAT SUNDAE DISH. DIP TWO LARGE SCOOPS OF CHOCOLATE ICE CREAM, AND COVER WITH COLD FUDGE SAUCE. GARNISH WITH WHIPPED CREAM.

– C.C. BROWN'S, LOS ANGELES, CALIFORNIA

A Pretty Movie Is Like a Sundae

In his book, "100 Nights in the Dark", critic Joe Barlow compared the Julia Roberts-Hugh Grant film, "Notting Hill", to a Hot Fudge Sundae: "It has no nutritional value whatsoever, but tastes so good going down that you simply don't care. And like our metaphoric Sundae, it leaves behind such a sweet aftertaste that you can't help wanting just a little more. Tooth decay be damned."

GETTING YOUR LICKS ON ROUTE 66

The Fair Oaks Pharmacy in South Pasadena has been located on Pasadena's Mission Street, part of the original Rte. 66, since 1915. And it's had its share of celebs—movie and football stars—getting in their Sundae licks. Yet one of the best-kept secrets in southern California is its old-fashioned malt Route 66 Sundae.

Drop one large scoop of vanilla ice cream and one large scoop of chocolate ice cream next to each other in a wide Sundae bowl. Cover both scoops with chocolate syrup and dust with malted milk powder. Finish with whipped cream and a maraschino on top.

– Fair Oaks Pharmacy, Pasadena, California

OREO SUNDAE

For those who want brownie points and their Sundae, too, the brownie is a popular base. The Oreo brownie is a Watson Drug twist on the I-want-it-all theme, although any wonderful brownie can be used in this recipe.

PLACE A 4-INCH SQUARE OREO BROWNIE (RECIPE FOLLOWS) AT THE CENTER OF A MEDIUM-SIZE PLATE. MORE THAN COVER WITH THREE SCOOPS OF VANILLA ICE CREAM, POUR HOT FUDGE SAUCE OVER THE ICE CREAM, TOP WITH WHIPPED CREAM AND SPRINKLE WITH CHOPPED PEANUTS.

OREO BROWNIE

5 ounces unsweetened chocolate
1/2 cup unsalted butter, softened
1 1/4 cups sugar
3 large eggs

2 teaspoons vanilla extract
1/2 cup all-purpose flour
Pinch of salt
12 Oreo cookies, coarsely chopped

PREHEAT OVEN TO 325 DEGREES. LINE A 10-INCH SQUARE BAKING PAN WITH ALUMINUM FOIL AND LIGHTLY OIL THE FOIL. PLACE CHOCOLATE IN A DOUBLE BOILER AND MELT UNTIL SMOOTH, ABOUT 3 MINUTES. USING AN ELECTRIC MIXER, BEAT BUTTER AND SUGAR IN LARGE BOWL UNTIL LIGHT AND FLUFFY, ABOUT 2 MINUTES. ADD EGGS, ONE AT A TIME, BEATING WELL AFTER EACH ADDITION. MIX IN MELTED CHOCOLATE AND VANILLA. ADD FLOUR AND SALT AND MIX ON LOW SPEED UNTIL COMBINED AND SMOOTH, ABOUT 2 MINUTES. WITH A RUBBER SPATULA, FOLD IN CHOPPED COOKIES. TRANSFER BATTER TO PREPARED PAN; SPREAD INTO AN EVEN LAYER WITH A RUBBER SPATULA. BAKE UNTIL A TOOTHPICK INSERTED IN THE CENTER COMES OUT CLEAN, 35-45 MINUTES. COOL ON WIRE RACK BEFORE CUTTING INTO 9 EQUAL PORTIONS.

– WATSON'S DRUG STORE, ORANGE, CALIFORNIA

Chapter 11

SODA JERK HALL OF FAME

🍒

"Don't I look like a film director?"

- JOHN LLOYD SULLIVAN (JOEL MCCREA)

"No, you look more like a soda jerk."

-A SHANTYTOWN HOBO

- *SULLIVAN'S TRAVELS* BY PRESTON STURGES

The soda fountain staff at the University of Michigan rebelled in 1938. Their issue: they didn't want to be called "jerks." Protesters organized the "Society for the Prevention of Cruelty to Soda Jerkers Who Want to be Known as Fountaineers of America."

It was a lost cause. They were jerks.

Time was when jerking was a prime job for young people on their way up. The pay wasn't much, but it was decent relative to other part-time gigs. More important, their workplace was the theater of Main Street America, and the jerks, in their starched white caps, were leading players in it. Here, they got to know and get known. Many a young man used the opportunity to attempt to woo the pretty young girls eating Sundaes. Others went beyond mastering the requisite ice cream mixing and Fountain Speak skills to test their jokes or their memories for faces. Although some few fountains hired female jerks—Lucille Ball, as I've mentioned, flubbed the job—in pre-liberated times soda jerking was usually a male game.

From the ranks of soda jerks have risen some of the country's well-known actors, politicians and orators.

Shortly after a ruddy-cheeked Bob Dole was voted best-looking boy in his high school by his female classmates, he got a job as soda jerk at Dawson's Drug Store on Main Street in his hometown of Russell, Kansas. At Dawson's he learned the power of having a good joke at hand

SUNDAES PLUS CRACKERS

Any true "fizzician" knew what cracker to prescribe with each type of Sundae. Salty crackers could accompany chocolate, coffee and malt flavors, but only a sweet cracker went with fruitier Sundaes. A glass of iced water was presented—and still should be—with each Sundae.

for the right customer, while developing a voracious appetite for Ice Cream Sundaes. "In my first two weeks on the job I put on nine pounds," remembered Dole after he'd become a U.S. Senator. Dole jerked before World War II swept him from Kansas toward injury and valor.

Leslie Townes Hope also jerked in the Midwest, albeit in earlier days. He made Sundaes at Hoffman's Ice Cream Parlor in Cleveland while he was in high school. By the time Pearl Harbor shattered American tranquility, citizens from coast to coast knew this former soda jerk as Bob Hope. Hope unstintingly contributed to the war effort as an entertainer of troops in every war theater.

Another Midwesterner, born Malcolm Little in Omaha, became a soda fountain clerk at Townsend Drug Store, in the Boston neighborhood of Roxbury, days after he'd quit work as a shoeshine "boy." Although his sister thought his new job a step up, Little, verging on age sixteen, had his reservations. When he'd become distinguished enough to write his autobiography, he recalled: "I put on the white jacket and started serving up sodas, sundaes, splits, shakes and all the rest of that fountain stuff to those fancy-acting Negroes."

Little's memoir is *The Autobiography of Malcolm X*. And in it, he remembers faithfully the years before he became the committed Black Nationalist and religious leader who founded the Nation of Islam.

Under young Malcolm's white jacket a sharp race-consciousness was in early, confused development, not yet at war with his somewhat reckless sense of fashion and fun. At night, he would toss aside his white jacket, don a "zoot suit" and head to Boston's Roseland Ballroom to dance the Lindy-hop and other steps, easily mastering the "flapping eagle," "kangaroo" and "split."

But he was serving at the drugstore when he met "soft" and "quiet" Laura, who turned out to be the best lindy partner of his life. "After a while, as soon as I saw her coming in," he wrote, "I'd start making a banana split. She was a real bug for them, and she came in every afternoon—after school. I imagine I'd been shoving that ice cream dish under her nose for five or six weeks before somehow it began to sink in that she wasn't like the rest . . . She always had some book with her, and poring over it, she would make a thirty-minute job of that daily dish of banana split."

It took some weeks more before Malcolm worked up the nerve to press his courtship by refusing to let Laura pay and giving her "extra ice cream." He was neither the first nor last soda jerk to attempt to win a heart this way. But he may have become the most painfully honest one. Malcolm and his banana-split girl became a Roseland item where, sad to say, he dumped her in favor of a blonde, whom he eventually blamed himself for destroying. Laura never returned to Townsend for another banana split, and Malcolm left off jerking to become a busboy at the Parker House.

Whether soda jerking was actually a calculated job choice for ambitious and personable young men or just a knee-jerk choice is hard to say. There were frequent job openings even before war carried young men to distant shores, because soda jerks left their posts and hometowns to go to college (which is what had created the Roxbury vacancy filled by the youth who would become Malcolm X), take steadier jobs or move to cities with more varied opportunities.

Among the future movie stars who might have been discovered (but weren't) as they poured hot fudge over ice cream were Tyrone Power, who jerked at a Cincinnati soda fountain (strategically located next to the Walnut Hills Orpheus movie house) and Gene Kelly, who jerked

FORCING
PUSHING
JAMMING
DOWN
That First Scoop
of Ice Cream
Into
the SUNDAE Glass
Means
OVER PORTIONS
and
LOSS

DEPRESSION ERA INSTRUCTIONS FOR SODA JERKS

ROMANTIC HERO

*R*emember Mr. Gower's drugstore and soda fountain in Frank Capra's holiday film, "It's a Wonderful Life"? George Bailey (Bobby Anderson) is the soda jerk trying to win the notice of Mary Hatch (Jean Gale), who sits at the counter. After she rejects his offer of coconut atop her Chocolate Sundae, George launches into a riff about where coconuts come from—Tahiti, Fiji, islands of the Coral Sea—and boasts that he plans to visit each exotic isle. He's got her but he doesn't know that because he can't hear her whisper, "George Bailey— I'll love you till the day I die."

on summer nights at Reymer's Candy, "home of the best Ice Creams in Pittsburgh." Gene didn't have much time to hoof it during summer sunlight, either, because he worked as a construction-company trucker six days per week, eight hours per day, at twenty-five cents an hour to put himself through Penn State. "I arrived in Hollywood twenty pounds overweight and as strong as an ox," he confessed, "so when I put on a white tie and tails like Astaire, I still looked like a truck driver."

Danny Kaye is another entertainer who did jerk time. "Life is a great big canvas," he once advised. "Throw all the paint on it you can." Kaye, a tailor's son, dropped out of school at age thirteen to work in New York's Catskill "Borscht Belt." With shtick and spritz, he became a clowning soda jerk while waiting for his big break. "You bet I arrived overnight," he once assured an interviewer. "Over a few hundred nights in the Catskills, vaudeville, in clubs and behind a soda fountain."

Joey Levitch, a.k.a. Jerry Lewis, also started working young. At fifteen, he was a professional lip-syncher when he could find a gig. When he couldn't, he retreated to the honored occupations of theatre usher and soda jerk.

Short, chubby Lou Costello jerked in Paterson, New Jersey, before teaming up with Bud Abbott as a vaudeville duo. Costello eventually reprised his soda-fountain role in the 1942 *Who Done It?*

As a struggling actor, Gene Hackman found rent money by work-

*Lou Costello (left) put in both real and reel (*Who Done It?*) soda jerk time.*

ing as a soda jerk and as a shoe salesman. Martin Sheen supplemented his stretch at the off-off-Broadway Living Theater with day jobs as a car-wash jockey and as a soda jerk.

Once, when a trekkie peppered Leonard Nimoy with technical questions about *Star Trek*, the exasperated star exclaimed, "For God's

GRACE UNDER PRESSURE

It was a soda jerk, worn out from hand-whipping heavy cream, who devised pressurized cans for spurting whip. In 1931, Charles Goetz, a beleaguered University of Illinois chemistry major, looked for a quick way to aerate cream. He succeeded by using gas to pressurize and release it as foam. The gas was the odorless, tasteless, non-flammable nitrous oxide used by dentists.

sake, it was only a television show!" Reality for Leonard once included soda jerking to pay for acting classes. Mark Hamill also supported his drama-class habit by scooping Sundaes. Then his Luke Skywalker role in *Star Wars* shot him to stardom.

Jazz icons Gene Krupa and Duke Ellington spent time on the fountain beat. During high school, Krupa jerked at a dance hall on Wisconsin Beach, north of Chicago, where he occasionally was allowed to fill in on the drums.

Ellington scooped in a D.C. establishment named The Poodle Dog Cafe. Ellington, who was introduced to the ivories by the Poodle Dog's pianist, listened to his tunes and learned them by ear. One evening when the pianist didn't show, the precocious soda jerk filled in. His repertoire wasn't big enough to fill the hours so he made it up as he went along. The Duke entitled his first composition, at age 14, "Soda Fountain Rag."

Writer Jack Kerouac's first loves were football and Sundaes. After he broke his leg carrying pigskin for Columbia, he convalesced with drinks and steaks, chased by double Hot Fudge Sundaes at the Lion's Den, a Morningside Heights student hangout.

After Jack hit the road, he briefly jerked in Washington, D.C., before heading west on his Beat adventures. Looking back, he wrote, "I rather

SUNDAE SEDUCTION

Soda Jerks had heart-winning techniques beyond dishing it up free, although tucking an extra scoop of ice cream in a Sundae for a pretty girl was a frequent ploy. The average jerk began by readjusting his starched cap, often jauntily cocking it to one side. The creative jerk might then attract the attention of winsome girls at the counter by fiddling with fixings to mock up a "new" Sundae combo, which he invited them to sample.

These carbonated cowboys dripped with both chocolate syrup and sex appeal, to hear some old-timers tell it.

Attraction, and sometimes victory, was signaled by a Sundae with two spoons.

THE CLINTON DRUG STORE, AS IT LOOKED WHEN HARRY TRUMAN JERKED THERE.

like the idea of having all my hours to myself: eating a Fudge Sundae, watching a movie, sleeping on my couch . . . all kinds of stuff that America brands 'shiftless.' "

Jerking was obviously too bourgeois an occupation for Kerouac. But not for newscaster David Brinkley who, in his autobiography, fondly recalls his soda-fountain days at Wrightsville Beach on a North Carolina barrier island. "For a schoolboy with a summer job at the beach making a little money working as a soda jerk . . . with girls all around in swimsuits that then seemed skimpy . . . it was heaven."

Jerking also had allure for Roy Halston, who dressed ice cream at the Merry-Go-Round Drive-In, located in Evansville, Indiana, before he dressed runway models.

The most famous former soda jerk of all is probably Harry S. Truman, 33rd President of the United States. Soda jerking was the job that shaped Harry while he was growing up in Independence, Missouri. Every morning, from seven o'clock until school time, he mopped the floor, cleaned away the trash and polished the prescription bottles at Jim Clinton's Drugstore on West Maple Street. On weekends, he made ice creams for the Sundaes he also constructed and served. Harry's salary was three dollars a week. "It was a great day all around when I got that three dollars," the plain-speaking president recalled.

Clinton's soda fountain has been preserved, with its six counter stools and eight tables, under walls lined with memorabilia and old photographs. All in all, the local historical society, which now runs Clinton's, does a bang-up job of making time travelers feel they are in yesteryear Kansas. Only the menu prices seem changed. Truman's weekly wage now buys one Sundae, with a little left over for the tip.

FRENCH PRESIDENTIAL HISTORY, TOO

Jacques Chirac spent one summer attending Harvard and working at a Boston ice cream fountain. "I was a soda jerk," he told Bill Clinton when the two dined together on foie gras and roasted lamb, accompanied by red wine, at Chez L'Ami Louis in Paris.

THE RECIPES

HARRY TRUMAN SUNDAE

This Sundae was Give-'Em-Hell-Harry's personal favorite when he had time to eat one.

•••

DIP ONE LARGE SCOOP OF CHOCOLATE ICE CREAM INTO A SUNDAE TULIP. COVER THE ICE CREAM WITH BUTTERSCOTCH SYRUP, GARNISH WITH WHIPPED CREAM AND PLACE A MARASCHINO CHERRY AT THE TOP.

•••

–CLINTON'S DRUGSTORE, INDEPENDENCE, MISSOURI

BACHELOR'S KISS

INTO A WIDE SUNDAE DISH, DIP ONE LARGE SCOOP OF CHOCOLATE ICE CREAM AND COVER WITH MARSHMALLOW SYRUP; THEN DIP ONE LARGE SCOOP OF VANILLA ICE CREAM AND COVER WITH HOT FUDGE SAUCE. LINE THE SIDES OF THE DISH WITH SLICES OF BANANA, GARNISH WITH WHIPPED CREAM, AND PLACE 2 MARASCHINO CHERRIES AT THE TOP.

– LAGOMARCINO CONFECTIONERY, MOLINE, ILLINOIS

VALENTINE SUNDAE

DIP ONE LARGE SCOOP OF VANILLA ICE CREAM INTO A SUNDAE TULIP. COVER THE ICE CREAM WITH A LADLEFUL OF CRUSHED STRAWBERRIES, GARNISH WITH WHIPPED CREAM, AND PLACE 5 OR 6 HEART-SHAPED CANDIES AROUND THE TOP.

– ROSELAND CANDY SHOP, CHICAGO, ILLINOIS

SWEETHEART SUNDAE

DIP 2 LARGE SCOOPS OF VANILLA ICE CREAM INTO A TALL SUNDAE GOBLET AND COVER THE ICE CREAM WITH MARSHMALLOW SYRUP, SHREDDED COCONUT AND CRUSHED CHERRIES. GARNISH WITH WHIPPED CREAM, AND PLACE A CHOCOLATE KISS AT THE TOP.

– HERSHEY DRUG STORE, HERSHEY, PENNSYLVANIA

Chapter 12

MAKING THE WORLD
SAFE FOR SUNDAES

*"The destiny of nations depends on the manner in
which they nourish themselves."*

— ANTHELME BRILLAT-SAVARIN

You just called it "The War." No number had to pass your lips. Loved ones waved tearful farewells as soldiers and sailors set out for duty in Europe or the South Pacific. A December 1941 *New Republic* editorial made the case emphatically: "The dirt farmer in the corn belt, the salesgirl behind the counter, the miner at the coal field, the stoker at sea—all believe in our democracy and demand vigorously that it be defended."

We still feel much the same way, to judge from the outpourings from our hearts since September 11, 2001.

Culture is not only the principles we live by. It is also, in large measure, what we live for.

We remember best those things we cherish. American troops needed a symbol for everything that was homebred, homemade and good about back home. Simple and innocent, ice cream stirred joyous recollections of the malt shop and hopes of reuniting with those waiting on the home front. Novelist Sarah Schulman once wrote, "Ice cream . . . a food that tastes so good in the mouth it makes a person feel human again. It brings back memories. It reminds a guy of other things."

Ice cream had become so identified with America that our Fascist enemies took heed. Japanese officials considered love of ice cream a sign of U.S. "decadence." Japanese vendors were forced to lower the prices for sodas and Sundaes, making them unprofitable to sell. In Italy, Mussolini outlawed the sale of ice cream altogether.

Although sugar was rationed in the States, ice cream and Sundaes

were too sacrosanct to be criticized. Citizens sacrificed other sweet pleasures first.

Puzzling over how to mix business with patriotism, in 1942 the Ice Cream Merchandising Institute, a promotional arm of the dairy industry, created a "Victory Sundae" advertising campaign. Participating merchants included a Defense Savings Stamp with every Ice Cream Sundae sold. Their slogan was "Keep 'Em Buying to Keep 'Em Flying."

The next year rationing began, which limited civilian purchases of sugar, milk and other dairy products.

Many restaurants closed, including several Howard Johnson franchises. The chain managed to stay afloat by serving commissary food to war workers and army recruits.

Canteens throbbed to the big-band recordings of Tommy Dorsey and Glenn Miller, and teens and servicemen could sometimes get Sundaes there. Spirits were also revived by the tones of the Andrews Sisters or bobby-soxer idol Frank Sinatra.

But splashy new civilian ice cream parlors were out of the question, not only because of ingredient shortages and lack of new equipment manufacturers of soda-fountain equipment were making airplane parts—but also because consumer extravagance suited neither our national economy or mood.

CHEESECAKE SUNDAE

"If I was sexy, I was just being me," said Betty Grable, referring to the pin-up showing off her legs (insured by Fox Studio for a million dollars). In this 1941 photo, the blonde actress, in a bathing suit and high heels, was positioned with her back to the camera, her smiling face looking over her right shoulder. Twenty thousand servicemen demanded copies in one week for bunker display.

Home-front soda jerks followed up with the Betty Grable Sundae, which consisted of cheesecake (of course), vanilla ice cream, raspberries in sauce, bananas and strawberries—topped with hot fudge, whipped cream and wet walnuts.

Army procurement policy ranked ice cream as essential to troop morale as soda pop and tobacco.

"Americans never quit," blustered General Douglas MacArthur. He wasn't talking about Sundaes, but he could have been, because the Army Quartermaster Corps was determined to provide our fighting men and women with the ingredients for Sundae facsimiles. Dehydrated ice cream mix was shipped to our bases around the world. Each soldier carried a ration of the powder, and once he followed instructions for making something resembling ice cream, he could turn it into a Sundae by adding canned fruit, crushed candy or any topping he could put his hands on. The temptation to horde sweets for Sundaes was great, since the ersatz ice cream needed whatever help it could get.

AN ADVERSISEMENT PUBLISHED IN THE SODA FOUNTAIN AND QUICK FOOD-SERVICE MAGAZINE, AUGUST, 1942.

Airmen on bombing missions sometimes placed a can of the cream mixture in the rear compartment of their B-29s. By the time they returned from a sortie (*if* they returned), high-altitude temperatures and the plane's vibrations had transformed the rude mix into ready-to-eat, cold ice cream.

Secretary of the Navy James Forrestal commissioned floating ice cream parlors to serve the troops—refrigerated barges with ice cream plants and a manufacturing capacity of up to ten gallons per second.

If you still don't believe Sundae ingenuity boosted morale and so helped win the war, then you haven't heard the story about Butch Baskin. Before the war, he'd run a small men's store inside Chicago's posh Palmer House Hotel. His shop provided formal wear for rich men; at the war's onset he attended to the dress needs of military officers.

After Baskin joined up, the Navy sent him to the South Seas, assigned to supply. Baskin was a genius at deciding what sailors most needed, and wheeling and dealing to get it. Butch bartered the company jeep for an ice cream freezer on a visiting aircraft carrier. The base didn't seem to miss its jeep, but all hopes were riveted on Baskin and the freezer. Butch rose to the challenge, doctoring up military-issue ice cream with local tropical fruits and exotic nuts. Baskin's wartime ice cream flavors made him a Pacific hero.

At the war's end, Baskin headed to Southern California to join his brother-in-law, Irv Robbins, who'd started an ice cream and frozen food store called Snowbird. Robbins didn't manufacture the ice cream he sold; he bought it and pasted on the Snowbird label.

Baskin jettisoned any notion of returning to haberdashery. He locked his future to Robbins and the siren call of ice cream. His first step was to bring the manufacture of ice cream home, and start adding some of those tropical flavors that had been such a wartime success.

Baskin and Robbins were operating six ice cream stores in the Los Angeles area by the time they dreamed up the "31" concept—an ice cream flavor for each day of the month. Each Baskin and Robbins location became a mini academy, furnished with old school desks and miniature pink tasting spoons so customers could try out new fresh fruit flavors.

By 1959, there were 500 Baskin-Robbins cafes, described by *Time* as "polka-dotted pleasure palaces."

The world had not only become safe again for Sundaes—Americans could joke about our excesses. On television, *Tonight Show* host Johnny Carson quipped, "My hometown of Norfolk, Nebraska, was so small, the Baskin-Robbins store only had two flavors."

A sign in front of a small church in Baltimore, Ohio (population 3,000), noted "We're not Baskin-Robbins, but our Sundays are divine."

And even Fidel Castro lightened up the Cold War with the boast that Cuba produced more ice cream flavors than its giant neighbor. Yeah, right. It didn't take long for Irv Robbins to phone *El Loco*'s Minister of Information to inform him that Baskin-Robbins alone had 290 varieties. Today there are 856 entries in the Baskin-Robbins flavor guide.

By the time the war ended, we'd come a long way from Thomas Jefferson's basic vanilla, but we were not yet done with combing the world for new flavors to be added to ice cream or toppings. Meanwhile, ice cream parlors across the seas had started copying the American Sundae. The Age of Sundae Imperialism had dawned.

THE RECIPES

MACARTHUR BLITZ SUNDAE

A prize-winning formula submitted to *Soda Fountain and Quick Food-Service* magazine in 1942.

• •

USE A TULIP SUNDAE GLASS. PLACE CHOCOLATE ICE CREAM ON BOTTOM, THEN VANILLA ICE CREAM ON TOP. CHOCOLATE SAUCE COVERS THE VANILLA. COVER ALL WITH SPANISH PEANUTS. NO OTHER TRIMMING NECESSARY.

• •

- HI-HUDDLE, ST. PAUL, MINNESOTA

WASHINGTON MONUMENT SUNDAE

*T*his is another tri-color Sundae born during World War II. If you plan on making one for the Fourth of July, you might find edible flags in an enterprising candy shop. But it's even more respectful to use decorative mini-flags.

• •

1 chocolate bomb (large scoop of chocolate)	Shot with chocolate sauce (1 1/2 ounces)
1 vanilla grenade (large scoop of vanilla)	Sprayed with salted peanuts (2 teaspoons of Spanish peanuts)

• •

DIP 5 SMALL SCOOPS OF VARIOUS-FLAVORED ICE CREAMS INTO A BANANA BOAT. CUT ONE LARGE BANANA INTO DISKS AND PLACE AROUND THE SIDE OF THE ICE CREAMS. LADLE ON 1/4 CUP CHOCOLATE SYRUP, 1/4 CUP RASPBERRY SYRUP, 1/4 CUP RASPBERRY SYRUP, AND 1/4 CUP CHOPPED WALNUTS IN MAPLE SYRUP. GARNISH WITH WHIPPED CREAM, AND SPRINKLE WITH RED, WHITE, AND BLUE JIMMIES. PLACE 5 SMALL AMERICAN FLAGS ALONG THE TOP.

- WOLFE'S SODA FOUNTAIN, WASHINGTON, D.C.

YANKEE DOODLE DANDY

𝒯his rousing Sundae shows the red, white and blue.

••

¼ cup marshmallow syrup
2 tablespoons crushed
   maraschino cherries

2 large scoops vanilla ice cream
2 tablespoons blueberries

••

POUR HALF OF THE MARSHMALLOW SYRUP INTO THE BOTTOM OF A WIDE SUNDAE GLASS, AND ADD THE ICE CREAM. TOP WITH THE REMAINDER OF THE MARSHMALLOW SYRUP AND PLACE THE CHERRIES ON ONE SIDE OF THE GLASS AND THE BLUEBERRIES ON THE OPPOSITE SIDE, LEAVING A WHITE STRIPE DOWN THE MIDDLE.

– CONGRESSIONAL DRUG STORE, WASHINGTON, D.C.

WAFFLE CONE SUNDAE

ℬutch Baskin kept up troop morale with his exotic-fruited ice creams and Sundaes, but the main creed he carried back home with him was freedom of choice.

••

PLACE TWO SMALL SCOOPS OF THE FLAVORS OF YOUR CHOICE INSIDE A WAF-FLE CONE. NEXT, POUR IN THE TOPPING OF YOUR CHOICE (HOT FUDGE, HOT CARAMEL, STRAWBERRY, PINEAPPLE, MARSHMALLOW OR CHOCOLATE SYRUP). GARNISH WITH WHIPPED CREAM, SPRINKLE WITH DICED ALMONDS, AND PLACE A MARASCHINO CHERRY ON THE TOP.

••

– BASKIN-ROBBINS, GLENDALE, CALIFORNIA

Chapter 13

HAPPINESS IS COFFEE ICE CREAM

"There's a fly in my ice cream."
- PATSY KELLY

"The flies here go in for winter sports."
- BERT LAHR

- *SING YOUR WORRIES AWAY* BY MONTE BRICE

*I*t was celebration time. Gone was any reason to stint on the best ingredients America had to offer. In 1948, Earle Swensen opened a modest ice cream parlor—nothing much to look at on the corner of Union and Hyde in San Francisco. But many found the full-bodied ice creams he served in his small place the best they'd tasted in years. He produced his ice cream in small batches, only twenty quarts at a time, and declared them as "good as father used to make."

Swensen was adept at many flavors, including coffee. There was nothing new about coffee ice cream; on its own, it had long been an upright American marriage of two favorite tastes. But giving coffee ice cream a prime Sundae role—now that was urbane. Whether it was the upscale Blum's ice cream parlors or Swensen's that first elevated coffee ice cream to the throne is a call hard to make these many years later. It seems almost inevitable, though, that San Francisco is the city where this happened.

I sometimes think of how especially hard it must have been for all those soldiers and sailors who'd shipped out from San Francisco. Even if they'd arrived only a day or two earlier, they'd have had time to leave a bit of their hearts in our most beautiful city.

For those lucky enough to live there, San Francisco had charms on offer beyond its hills dotted with painted-lady houses, which looked down into gardens or across to the sparkling Pacific or bay. San Francisco was

HIPPIE HEAVEN

*B*ud's ice cream parlor had been lolling around San Francisco since 1932 when the Hippie generation happened upon its wholesome virtues in the late 1960s. And even though Bud's was over 30, the flower children trusted the restorative powers of its signature concoction, a massive scoop of vanilla between two enormous oatmeal cookies. Syrups (strawberry, pineapple, hot fudge and others) could be ladled on.

The flower children reluctantly aged into adults and Bud's moved on, too, to upscale Laguna Beach, California and to Kuala Lumpur, Malaysia, transforming into Bud's Ice Cream of San Francisco where Sundaes are the star dishes.

Bud's, like most of its onetime brethren in the Bay Area (and throughout North America, for that matter) has kept up with the times by also pushing frozen yogurt; Bud's calls it "Yogurt Ice Cream".

A survey of the hundreds of establishments in California coastal towns, which categorize themselves as ice cream parlors shows that the majority of them either have names celebrating the sophistication of their desserts, as in Gelato Factory, or their luxurious healthiness: Golden Spoon Frozen Yogurt. (Both have multiple locations.) For wit, the prize goes to the singular Humphrey Yogurt in Costa Mesa.

a "foodie" town before the term was invented to describe people who take a serious interest in cuisine. Sourdough bread, Dungeness crab, a variety of pastas and delicate Chinese food were at hand there before much of America knew of such delights. Sophisticated San Franciscans quietly thought they lived in a city possibly rivaled only by Paris. And if Paris had its *frappē* (iced coffee with a scoop of vanilla), well, San Francisco had its coffee ice cream marvels.

San Francisco native Nina Pinsky can still remember, and very nearly taste, the "Cof-fiesta" Sundaes she enjoyed at Blum's when she was a girl. They were made with coffee ice cream, chocolate sauce (*salsa de cacao*, as the menu had it) and a whipped cream so rich and flavorful it was called Charlotte Russe. The whole thing was then generously sprinkled with "koffee krunch," chewy bits of coffee-flavored honeycomb crunch (which Blum's also used as a cake topping). This Sundae, as the menu described it, was topped with the "ubiquitous *cereza mar-*

THIS SUNDAE MAKER IMAGE WAS ON THE BACK COVER OF THE BLUM'S MENU.

rasquina," that is, a maraschino cherry. It's the coffee crunch that makes this Sundae so special.

Another Blum's special was the Scheherezade Sundae, which exotically paired coffee ice cream swathed in caramel sauce with raspberry ice bathed in marshmallow sauce. The cherry atop the Scheherezade was a "maraschino ruby."

Blum's had four San Francisco locations, a sprinkling of other California branches and eastern outposts in Lord & Taylor stores. San Francisco's Fairmont Hotel housed a small but memorable version with a fountain and a few classic wrought-iron ice-cream tables and chairs. The main Blum's establishment, at Polk and California, had booths. It offered sandwiches for those who insisted; they could be found listed on the menu *after* three pages of ice cream delights. Blum's was a magnet for San Franciscans in the know: a place for older couples after a night on the town as well as a date magnet, and an afternoon spot for families and shoppers craving a Sundae fix.

All and all, an hour at Blum's was a happy-times-are-here-again affair.

Swensen also had a flair for naming Sundaes. His coffee-ice cream creations, Irish Coffee Macarooney and Gold Rush, remain on the menu.

Swensen sold his name to franchise managers in 1964. There are now more than three hundred shops worldwide, but Earle's daughters have held on to the original at the foot of Russian Hill. And it remains a Mecca for lovers of ice cream.

Blum's, however, is gone forever except in fond memory.

The best Sundae place in San Francisco today is arguably the Ghirardelli Chocolate Manufactory and Soda Fountain, whose brick walls have been perfumed with roasting cocoa beans for over a century. The dream started with Italian-born Domingo Ghirardelli, who'd lingered amidst the cocoa trees of Guatemala before sailing to California. The manufactory's soda fountain whips up a world-class Hot Fudge "Bonanza" Sundae, which can be made with "Turkish Coffee Ice Cream" if you so choose.

"The Rock," a chocolate-armored vanilla island in a whipped cream bay, is as formidable as Alcatraz before it became a tourist site. Rivers of chocolate syrup running over three marshmallow-covered chocolate ice cream scoops, studded with nuts and chocolate nuggets, mark a Sundae well named "Strike It Rich."

THE RECIPES

COFFEE CRUNCH

𝐵lum's "Koffee Crunch" was the extra topping that drove San Francisco Sundae-lovers wild. You'll need a candy thermometer to prepare the crunch perfectly. To re-create "Cof-fiesta," generously sprinkle the coffee crunch over a Sundae composed of coffee ice cream, chocolate sauce, whipped cream and a maraschino on top. It's javalicious!

Unflavored vegetable oil (for greasing baking pan)	1/4 cup strong brewed coffee
1 tablespoon baking soda	1 1/2 cups sugar
	1/4 cup light corn syrup

GENEROUSLY OIL A LARGE BAKING SHEET. SIFT BAKING SODA ONTO A SHEET OF WAXED PAPER AND SET NEARBY. COMBINE COFFEE, SUGAR AND CORN SYRUP INTO A HEAVY 4-QUART SAUCEPAN. PLACE THE SAUCEPAN OVER MEDIUM HEAT, STIRRING OCCASIONALLY UNTIL SUGAR DISSOLVES. WHEN COFFEE MIXTURE IS CLEAR AND BEGINS TO BOIL, INCREASE HEAT TO MEDIUM-HIGH. USING A CANDY THERMOMETER, MONITOR THE TEMPERATURE OF THE MIXTURE CAREFULLY. AS THE MIXTURE APPROACHES 270-280 DEGREES F., BE SURE TO STIR OCCASIONALLY IN ORDER TO PREVENT IT FROM SCORCHING OR BECOMING OVERLY FOAMY.

WHEN THE MIXTURE REACHES 290 DEGREES, REMOVE THE SAUCEPAN FROM THE HEAT AND STIR IN THE BAKING SODA. THIS WILL CAUSE THE MIXTURE TO FOAM FIERCELY. WHILE IT'S STILL FOAMING, POUR THE MIXTURE ONTO THE OILED BAKING SHEET. DO NOT SPREAD. ALLOW THE COFFEE CRUNCH MIXTURE TO COOL FOR AT LEAST ONE HOUR.

ONCE COOL, WRAP THE CRUNCH IN A CLEAN KITCHEN TOWEL OR PLASTIC BAG, AND, USING A ROLLING PIN OR OTHER HEAVY UTENSIL, CRUSH THE CRUNCH INTO VERY SMALL (PEBBLE-SIZED) PIECES. STORE THE CRUNCH IN AN AIRTIGHT CONTAINER UNTIL YOU'RE READY TO USE IT. MAKES ABOUT 3 CUPS.

THREE OF SWENSEN'S BEST

IRISH COFFEE MACAROONEY

Dip 2 large scoops of coffee ice cream into a tall Sundae goblet. Smother with crushed macaroons, garnish with whipped cream, and place a maraschino cherry at the top.

BLACK BART SUNDAE

Dip one large scoop of chocolate ice cream into a tall Sundae goblet and cover with marshmallow sauce. Then add one large scoop of vanilla ice cream and blanket with hot fudge sauce. Top with whipped cream, sprinkle with sliced almonds, and finish with a cherry.

GOLD RUSH

Dip one large scoop of chocolate ice cream into a tall Sundae goblet and cover with hot fudge sauce. Add one large scoop of coffee ice cream and cover with hot butterscotch sauce. Garnish with a sprinkle of sliced almonds and whipped cream. Top with a maraschino.

– Swensen's, San Francisco, California

Chapter 14

SUNDAES GO SOFT

"He was adept at finding open receivers, not-so-open receivers and receivers covered like chocolate syrup on a D.Q. [Dairy Queen] Sundae."

– SPORTSWRITER JESS NICHOLAS

Both Sundaes and their eaters reinvented themselves in the bustling postwar years. Masses of Americans, aided by the G.I. Bill, moved out of city rentals to the under-construction suburbs, where most of the compact new houses had garages or, at least, short driveways ending in parking pads. Many Americans also left the farm or rural towns where they'd been raised. In short, Americans moved into their cars and their Sundaes met them on the road.

The neighborhood drugstore soda fountain became a less popular meeting place as people scattered to new homes and new jobs out of its orbit. The weekday lunch or afternoon Sundae break on Main Street began losing its hold on our routine.

Even young housewives, who theoretically might have had the time for a Sundae afternoon outing, in reality did not. They gave birth young to their 2.5 babies—and in quick succession. Many no longer lived within walking distance of drugstores, candy stores or coffee shops.

Nowadays, the "soccer mom" has her own car to run errands and chauffeur her youngsters to their appointed rounds. But back in the '50s and '60s, most families had only one car that the bread earner (almost always the husband) drove to work or left at the train station. The suburban mother's social life consisted of a cup of coffee in her kitchen or in her neighbor's, while they kept their eyes on the kids.

Sundaes belonged to the weekend. In *Familiar Territory*, Joseph Epstein observes, "the Sunday drive usually had no greater goal than a longish ride for an ice cream soda or Sundae."

The most innovative existing ice-cream businesses were the first to get the idea.

FRISCO COMEBACK KID

Mel Weiss and Harold Dobbs opened a carhop eatery in San Francisco in 1947, which was successful enough to spawn ten northern California offspring. But two decades later, the chain, outdone by bigger competitors, yelled uncle.

The first Mel's was scheduled for demolition when George Lucas discovered it and decided to use it as the centerpiece of his teen movie, "American Graffiti". It remained standing long enough to take its star turn. But Mel Weiss's son, Steven, opened a new Mel's Drive In thirteen years later, in 1985, on Lombard Street. The carhops are gone, but you can still order from a basic burger-and-fries menu in a 1950s vintage chrome-and-formica setting.

Mel's signature "Deluxe" Sundae is a classic black and white treat: two large scoops each of vanilla and chocolate go under the chocolate syrup, whipped cream and cherry.

Thomas Andreas Carvelas had Americanized his name to Tom Carvel when he opened an ice cream store on Central Park Avenue in Hartsdale, New York, in 1934. One day, when his Model A Ford broke down while he was making a delivery, his ice cream started to melt. Thinking quickly, he offered it up in some borrowed dishes to passers-by. Carvel noticed that customers seemed to enjoy the softness of the not-so-frozen dessert. In 1936, he was awarded a patent for a "no air pump" low-temperature ice cream machine. In 1947, Carvel created a franchise for his soft-serve ice cream and a "Sundae School" training program for store managers.

A quickly expanding number of Carvel outlets—compact glass-fronted buildings with pitched roofs—appeared on road setbacks that left sufficient room in front for cars to pull in. A whole family might spill from the car to watch the Carvel ice cream swirl into paper cups or cones, or one or two designates might go to the stand window with varied orders. And it wasn't only families who skidded to a stop at the roadside ice cream shrines. When Junior could wrest away Dad's keys to the family Chevrolet or Ford, chances are he and his date, or a whole car-full of kids, stopped for ice cream. Many Carvel Sundaes were-and are consumed in vehicles. One only hopes the driver settles for a cone, safely getting in his licks as he drives away.

A similar soft-serve success story is rooted in Illinois, where J.F. McCullough and his son, Alex, arranged to test their own soft product in an ice cream retail shop in Kankakee owned by Sherb Noble. Noble advertised an "All You Can Eat for 10 Cents" sale one August afternoon in 1938 that drew a crowd of 1,600 men, women and children, all clamoring to try the new ice cream.

It must have been an exhilarating but trying day for the McCulloughs (not to mention Noble's customers), because serving so much soft ice cream was such a slow, drawn-out process.

The McCulloughs and Noble couldn't seriously market the new product until they discovered a new-type freezer, invented by Harry Oltz of Hammond, Indiana, which was capable of producing a continuous flow of softer ice cream. Understandably, the senior McCullough considered the freezer a prize cow and took to referring to it as "the Queen." Equipped with the Queen, Noble opened a store in Joliet, Illinois, dedicated to selling the soft ice cream it easily dispensed. The store was named Dairy Queen.

In 1955, a family out for a Sunday drive without a Carvel stand in sight might satisfy their Sundae yens at a Dairy Queen, which by then had 2,600 locations.

Crusty old-timers who say Americans began to go soft in the prosperous 1950s are confusing people with the fluffy desserts that became so popular in that era.

THE SOFT-SERVE SUNDAE BECAME A FAVORITE IN THE 1950S.

HOW MUCH ICE CREAM CAN ONE COUNTRY EAT?

*A*fter the turn of the 19th century, Americans ate about three quarts of ice cream per capita, annually. Before the second World War, we devoured almost 10 quarts, with this number rising to almost 15 quarts in 1945, in celebration of both victory and an increasing number of freezers.

In recent years, over one and a half billion gallons of ice cream have been produced each year in the United States, reports Lynda Utterback, editor of National Dipper, "enough to fill the Grand Canyon." This works out to 23.77 quarts for each of us, about a third of which is consumed at home.

"Vanilla ice cream has always and will always be the most popular flavor," Ms. Utterback continues, "because most Sundaes start with vanilla."

THE RECIPES

JACK AND JILL SUNDAE

*J*ack and Jill and their parents drove up the hill, one fine evening in 1955, to fetch classic Sundaes—only these were made with soft ice cream and served in small, coated cardboard pails.

FILL A SUNDAE CUP WITH SOFT VANILLA ICE CREAM TO FORM A PEAK. PUMP CHOCOLATE SYRUP DOWN ONE SIDE OF THE ICE CREAM, AND PUMP MARSH-MALLOW SYRUP DOWN THE OTHER. PLACE A MARASCHINO CHERRY ON TOP.

– DAIRY QUEEN

Chapter 15

WHERE SUNDAE TIME STANDS STILL

*"Try to cut back.
Leave the cherry off your Hot Fudge Sundae."*

–GARFIELD IN *WORDS TO THE WIDE* BY JIM DAVIS

"All Shook Up" played on jukeboxes, and the whoosh of a whipped-cream nozzle was also music to our ears. Rock and Roll seemed to energize the soda fountain in the 1950s, our last era of eating innocence. It was a great time for Tom's Ice Cream Bowl in Zanesville, Ohio.

Three scoops in a soup bowl—that's how former astronaut and U.S. Senator John Glenn describes his favorite Sundae at Tom's. Glenn, who grew up in nearby New Concord, still drives to Tom's for a Hot Fudge Sundae when he visits home.

Zanesville, in southeastern Ohio, was named after Ebenezer Zane, the great-grandfather of Zane Grey. The novelist was born in a seventeen-room Victorian in Zanesville in 1875, which is the town's *other* claim to fame.

When Glenn was a boy, the town's main thoroughfare led right up to the front door of Tom's Ice Cream Bowl on Maple Street. But an access ramp to the Interstate has cut off that end of Maple, so nowadays you wind tightly around the bumpy brick streets to get to the Ice Cream Bowl.

It's worth the detour. As you enter through the swinging double doors, you see yellow Formica-top tables, each surrounded by four chrome chairs, upholstered in well-worn green leatherette. Ten matching stools at the counter face three stark mirrors. The floor is industrial terrazzo, and walls are shiny block tiles in a two-tone combination of cream and turquoise.

Ten years ago, an urban sophisticate might have called the look "tired." Now it's effortlessly "retro-chic." Truth is, nobody in his right mind comes to Tom's Ice Cream Bowl to gawk at its furnishings. You come to eat a Sundae.

There is hardly an aroma in the world more appetizing than the scent of warm nuts right out of the oven, and this is the enchanting smell that permeates Tom's. A wooden counter displays freshly-roasted cashews, peanuts, redskins and Spanish nuts. You can eat them plain or ask for your favorites on your Sundae.

Tom's does not, praise be, fancy up the ice cream. There is no whipped cream here. There's not even a maraschino cherry in sight. You could argue that the cherry has been an identifying mark of the Sundae right from the start. And, of course, you'd be right. But the Sundaes at Tom's don't *need* cherries. Good ice cream and hot-fudge sauce, plus nuts—that's the deal, plain and simple. As manager Joe Baker tells it, "We don't want anything to get in the way of the nuts."

Baker has been at Tom's since his own high school days. Attired in white shirt, bow tie, and paper hat, he appears younger than his 39 years, while also looking as if he just stepped out of a Norman Rockwell painting. Even with a hard-working corps of trained clerks—as the soda jerks are now called here—he claims he's still the best. And Joe teaches each new clerk the time-honored craft of making a Sundae *right*: "First we teach each apprentice the art of hand-dipping, and it is indeed an art.

You have to be fast. You must go down and come up with the right portion in one dip," says Baker. "Only then do you move up to the fountain to make Sundaes." With a smile, Baker adds that what he teaches younger people is "frozen dessert technology."

Baker is also the chief ice cream maker and is especially proud of his creamy vanilla. His uses colorless, natural vanilla extract to produce a bright white ice cream with the moderate butterfat content he believes best suits Sundaes. Joe keeps track. He has personally made 368,000 gallons of ice cream during his twenty-two years of service.

The shop is named for six-foot-four, 260-pound Tom Mirgon, who had made ice cream at the local Hemmer Dairy before he and a partner launched out on their own in 1948. Some in Zanesville remember Tom's deep, booming voice preaching cleanliness, good service and fair prices. "If you do that," Tom would say, "they'll find you no matter where you're located."

In 1953, the year that Mirgon bought out his partner, a customer complained that Tom's generous portions overflowed the tulip glass as soon as he put his spoon in it: "Why don't you put this damn thing in a soup bowl so I can eat it?" the customer suggested. From that day on, Sundaes were served in bowls.

When Bill Sullivan bought the business from Mirgon in 1984, he inherited a place that looked like Ozzie and Harriet might walk in at any moment. Sullivan was either smart enough or stubborn enough not to change a thing. "The longer we're here, and the longer we keep it the same, the more of an institution we become," Sullivan explains.

Lunchtime regulars start pouring into Tom's at 11:15 a.m. The customers wave or say hello to one another; the clerks know the names of most.

"I'm not going to get too much, considering I've had a late breakfast," says 14-year-old Kimberly Schoenbrunn, who is visiting Zanesville from nearby Cambridge.

"You can get anything you want," replies her grandfather, whose treat this is.

When the server comes over to her table, she orders a cup of chili and a three-scoop banana split.

Mr. and Mrs. George Whelan, a retired insurance agent and his wife, live in the neighborhood. "Most of the choices are just too much for our small appetites," says Mrs. Whelan, "so we share a Pineapple Sundae."

"It's our favorite," agrees her husband, who has been a Tom's customer for forty years. The couple finishes every bit of their dessert,

OTHERWISE KNOWN AS BUCKEYES

*T*om's is nothing but a squalling baby, compared to its great-great uncle, Wittich's Candy, in Circleville, Ohio. Wittich's has been making residents of the Buckeye State happy since 1840, so it's altogether fitting that it has the honor of the Buckeye Sundae. The buckeye is an inedible variety of horse chestnut, but Wittich has gotten around this inconvenience by creating a "buckeye" candy made of chocolate and peanut butter to top its Sundae. The Wittich Buckeye Sundae maker covers vanilla ice cream with hot fudge sauce, and chocolate peanut-butter ice cream with peanut butter sauce. Yum!

Wittich Candy's confection recipes are top secret, but you can approximate the Buckeye Sundae with similar syrups and a chocolate-peanut or chocolate-peanut-butter candy. Better yet, follow your sweet tooth and find your way to Circleville, half an hour's drive due south of Columbus.

then purchases a quarter-pound of blanched peanuts for the walk home.

"There is something quite extraordinary about hot fudge drizzled down a pile of vanilla, then topped with warm, salted cashews," observes Mike Sidley, a paper supply salesman from Erie, Pennsylvania, who stops off Interstate 70 whenever his calls take him near Zanesville. "I'll gladly drive out of my way to visit Tom's."

Another 1950s place I hear that people go out of their way to visit is Nau's on West Lynn Street in downtown Austin, Texas. The official name is Nau's Enfield Pharmacy, but everyone just calls it Nau's. Since 1951, Nau's has hardly changed a thing. Rumor is that some Texas lawmakers show up in Austin only because it's an excuse for a Pineapple Sundae at Nau's.

On a *bigger* scale than Nau's—sorry, Texans, but it's true—is Junior's in Brooklyn, born on Election Day, 1951. Hold on, New Yorkers,

I know what you're thinking: You don't go to Junior's for the Sundaes; you go for the heartburn.

Okay, okay—Brooklynites and all the people who've ever lived in the borough return for the matzoh ball soup, fried chicken and the best cheesecake on the planet.

But some Junior's cognoscenti go for the "Mountain High Sundaes," drenched in syrup and whipped cream, which really are worth knowing *from*, providing you haven't eaten everything else on the menu first.

Junior's, which has been owned by the Rosen family for three generations, still has a long fountain, lined with fifteen stools, along with its bright orange Naugahyde booths and dozens of tables. The restaurant is so large a legend that it probably can't be held up as typical of the 1950s or anything else. Nonetheless, it ought to be a place of pilgrimage for Sundae lovers. But those who aren't going to get to Brooklyn any time soon can make its famed hot fudge sauce at home.

This short tale of old-timers in no way exhausts the list of establishments across the country that will put you in mind of the way it was—while serving very good Sundaes in the here and now. And in the pages to come, I'll be exploring more.

But there are also ice cream parlors, which, while not technically of a ripe old age, have done a darn good job of recreating Eisenhower-era feeling or that from longer ago. Hoppie's, for example, in Oxford, New York, is equipped and furnished with a vintage Bastian Blessing bobtail soda fountain that still makes ice cream sodas the old-fashioned way—with a stream of soda water strong enough to leave ice cream on the ceiling if the preparer is not careful. Hoppie's also has an old-fashioned will to please. Proprietors David and MaryEl Emerson promise flat out on their website "to make your ice cream dreams come true . . . if you're not happy, you don't pay."

Sundaes and the ambiences in which they flourish so sum up America that there are hundreds, if not thousands, of old-fashioned establishments nationwide, along with newcomers in every guise. I haven't tasted every Sundae in America (no one could), although Lord knows I've tried.

THE RECIPES

PEANUT BUTTER SAUCE

1 cup smooth or chunky peanut
butter

¹/₄ cup light corn syrup

¹/₂ cup heavy cream or sweetened condensed milk

COMBINE INGREDIENTS IN A SAUCEPAN OVER LOW HEAT, STIRRING UNTIL WARM AND THICK BUT NOT GUMMY. IF THE SAUCE THICKENS TOO MUCH, THIN TO DESIRED CONSISTENCY WITH ADDITIONAL CREAM OR CONDENSED MILK. SERVE WARM.

SAUCE CAN BE REFRIGERATED IN AN AIRTIGHT CONTAINER FOR UP TO 3 WEEKS. TO RE-HEAT, MICROWAVE AT 15-SECOND INTERVALS UNTIL WARM. MAKES 1 ¹/₂ CUPS.

NUTTY DELIGHTS FROM ZANESVILLE

TIN ROOF

DIP 2 LARGE SCOOPS OF VANILLA ICE CREAM INTO AN 8-OUNCE SOUP BOWL. LADLE 4 OUNCES CHOCOLATE SYRUP OVER THE TOP, AND COMPLETELY COVER WITH ONE LAYER OF FRESH-ROASTED SPANISH PEANUTS. PLACE BOWL ON A SAUCER AND SERVE.

BLACK AND WHITE

DIP 3 LARGE SCOOPS OF VANILLA ICE CREAM INTO AN 8-OUNCE SOUP BOWL. LADLE ON 2 OUNCES OF CHOCOLATE SYRUP, THEN LADLE ON 2 OUNCES OF MARSHMALLOW SYRUP. PLACE BOWL ON A SAUCER AND SERVE.

PEANUT BUTTER SUNDAE

DIP 2 LARGE SCOOPS OF VANILLA ICE CREAM INTO AN 8-OUNCE SOUP BOWL. LADLE 4 OUNCES OF A CARAMEL SAUCE/PEANUT BUTTER BLEND OVER THE TOP. PLACE BOWL ON A SAUCER AND SERVE. (TO RECREATE TOM'S TOPPING, MIX 1 CUP

OF WARM CLASSIC CARAMEL SYRUP WITH $^3/_4$ CUP OF CHUNKY PEANUT BUTTER AND $^1/_8$ TEASPOON SALT, IF USING NO-SALT PEANUT BUTTER).

– TOM'S ICE CREAM BOWL, ZANESVILLE, OHIO

TEXAS PINEAPPLE SUNDAE

PLACE ONE HEAPING SPOONFUL OF CRUSHED FRESH PINEAPPLE AT THE BOTTOM OF A SUNDAE TULIP. DIP 2 LARGE SCOOPS OF VANILLA ICE CREAM INTO THE GLASS AND COVER WITH 2 HEAPING SPOONFULS OF CRUSHED PINEAPPLE. GARNISH WITH WHIPPED CREAM, AND PLACE A MARASCHINO CHERRY AT THE TOP.

– NAU'S ENFIELD PHARMACY, AUSTIN, TEXAS

P, B & J SUNDAE

DIP TWO SCOOPS OF VANILLA ICE CREAM INTO A TALL GOBLET AND DRIZZLE WITH PEANUT-BUTTER SAUCE. COVER WITH YOUR CHOICE OF RASPBERRY, BLUEBERRY OR STRAWBERRY TOPPING. SANCTIFY WITH WHIPPED CREAM AND A MARASCHINO CHERRY.

– HOPPIE'S, OXFORD, NEW YORK

MOUNTAIN HIGH HOT FUDGE SUNDAE

JUNIOR'S HOT FUDGE SAUCE

$^1/_2$ cup unsalted butter
$^3/_4$ cup unsweetened cocoa powder
2 ounces bittersweet chocolate, chopped

$^1/_4$ teaspoon salt
1 14-ounce can sweetened condensed milk
$^1/_2$ cup heavy cream
1 tablespoon pure vanilla extract

MELT THE BUTTER IN A SMALL SAUCEPAN OVER MEDIUM HEAT. STIR IN THE COCOA, CHOCOLATE, AND SALT AND COOK UNTIL THE CHOCOLATE MELTS. SLOWLY STIR IN THE MILK AND CREAM, AND HEAT UNTIL THE SAUCE IS SMOOTH AND WARM. STIR THE SAUCE CONSTANTLY, AND WATCH IT CAREFULLY SO IT DOES NOT BOIL OR STICK TO THE BOTTOM OF THE PAN. REMOVE THE SAUCE FROM THE HEAT AND WHISK IN THE VANILLA. SERVE HOT OVER ICE CREAM.

HOT FUDGE MAY BE REFRIGERATED IN AN AIRTIGHT CONTAINER FOR UP TO 3 WEEKS. TO RE-HEAT, SET OVER A DOUBLE BOILER, WHISKING VIGOROUSLY UNTIL FUDGE REGAINS ITS CREAMY TEXTURE. IF RE-HEATING OVER DIRECT HEAT, USE VERY LOW FLAME, AND BE CAREFUL NOT TO LET THE SAUCE BUBBLE OR BURN. MAKES 2 CUPS.

HEAT THE HOT FUDGE SAUCE JUST UNTIL IT'S EASY TO STIR AND WARM TO THE TOUCH.

WHEN PREPARING THE SUNDAE, MAKE SURE THE ICE CREAM IS FROZEN SOLID; IF IT SCOOPS OUT OF THE CARTON VERY EASILY, IT'S TOO SOFT.

DIP ONE LARGE SCOOP OF VANILLA ICE CREAM INTO A LARGE SUNDAE GOB-LET, AND COVER WITH A GENEROUS AMOUNT OF HOT FUDGE SAUCE. THEN ADD ANOTHER LARGE SCOOP OF VANILLA AND SPOON OVER MORE SAUCE. REPEAT UNTIL THE SUNDAE STANDS "MOUNTAIN HIGH" OVER THE TOP OF THE GLASS. USING A PASTRY BAG FITTED WITH A LARGE FLUTED TIP, PIPE A MOUNTAIN OF WHIPPED CREAM ON TOP, THEN PLACE A BING CHERRY AT THE TOP.

– JUNIOR'S, BROOKLYN, NEW YORK

Chapter 16

SUNDAES
IN NEW YORK

🍒

"I once read a silly fairy tale, called The Three Princes of Serendip: as their highnesses traveled, they were always making discoveries, by accidents and sagacity, of things they were not in quest of."

–HORACE WALPOLE (IN A LETTER TO HORACE MANN)

Some restaurants are ahead of their of time. Serendipity 3, in Manhattan, established in 1954 as a whimsical clothing/antiques boutique and ice cream parlor, is such a place. Today, it is one of few places for original Sundaes in Manhattan, but it had brilliant competition when it started; Rumpelmayer's and Schrafft's were the most glittering.

In their book, *On the Town in New York*, Michael and Ariane Batterberry report that in 1891 there were more soda fountains than bars in Gotham. In the 1950s and '60s, that could still appear true to the young at heart.

It's not often that New Yorkers cry into their Ice Cream Sundaes, but it's not a sweet sorrow for the Sundae faithful of Manhattan to part with the likes of Hicks, Rumpelmayer's, The Flick and Schrafft's, not to mention the corner soda fountains that were once a staple of every neighborhood.

Rumpelmayer's, tucked into the St. Moritz on Central Park South, is likely most missed when Rockefeller Center is alight with its Christmas Tree or in the first feckless days of summer.

For three decades, fashionable New York couples with equally fashionable children, dressed by Best & Co., flocked to elegant, respectable Rumpelmayer's, with its mirrored walls and stylish mosaics. They came for its ice cream, accompanied by a French fan biscuit, all served in impeccable dishes on tables set with white cloths. A Rumpelmayer's

MUCH BESIDES GLORIOUS SUNDAES IS FOR SALE AT SERENDIPITY 3.

Sundae approached necessity before or after a performance of *Nutcracker Suite*. It was also where Fifth and Park Avenue parents kissed off their children before they left for summer camp.

For families from Elsewhere, visiting during school vacations, Rumpelmayer's was a *must* stop after a sweep through the lobby of the Plaza, the hotel where Eloise, the most spoiled little girl in literature, forever lives.

Horse cabs still wait for romantics across the street from where Rumpelmayer's stood, on real estate that finally became too desirable to support even the classiest ice cream joint. Families in search of a Sundae experience these days usually head east to Serendipity 3, near Bloomingdale's. The "3" in the name is not serendipitous; it signifies the number of founding partners.

The artist, Andy Warhol, discovered Serendipity 3 before the world discovered him. Fresh from Pittsburgh, he took to sipping espresso and devouring Sundaes at this unorthodox café, with its odd merchandise and stained-glass lampshades. Warhol also loved Woolworth's Sundaes, as you already know, and he proclaimed affection for Schrafft's, but it's easy to see why a man who abhorred dullness would fall in love with loopy Serendipity. Besides, its owner let Warhol settle his tab in drawings. The pink corner table in Serendipity's dining area became an intersection for the many vectors of pop culture. Each time Warhol appeared, he seemed to bring more and odder friends.

Even after Warhol and his crowd made his Union Square "Factory" their headquarters, Serendipity 3 remained one of his destinations. Andy couldn't keep away from parties; he went to several most nights, and Serendipity 3 was and is almost a party in itself.

You bounce inside to a setting that is at once mysterious and familiar, filled with a jumble of treasures and trash. You can't miss the huge clock, rescued from a demolition site around the corner. Try on a Garbo hat and maribou-trimmed dress, fondle a cross-eyed calico rooster and sniff a cucumber soap before you sit down to an equally eclectic menu, or vice versa. The food choices might include filet

OPENING NIGHT SUNDAES

These two are for your "Playbill," from Serendipity 3's exotic creations, which you are not likely to be able to duplicate at home unless you have an artistic temperament, a confectioner's skills, some unusual molds, a stock of food coloring and a hypodermic needle.

SOUND OF MUSIC

A marshmallow snow-capped mountain of mint chocolate chip ice cream, with a waterfall of peanut butter topping, all sitting in a field of green whipped cream, chocolate musical notes, variously-colored candy blossoms and a marzipan "Maria."

ROCKY HORROR/SWEET TRANSVESTITE

A lurid, rocky road of 5 scoops of chocolate ice cream studded with chocolate chunks, cross-dressed with marshmallow and almonds, accessorized with red and black licorice whips. "Touch-a-Touch-a-Touch Me" with a flourish of "Magenta" whipped cream, topped with a gummy "Frank 'n' Furter."

"Riff Raff" will inject the creation with a syringe filled with blood-red raspberry sauce.

mignon, rhubarb omelet or hotdogs, but you can be sure that "Drugstore Sundaes" will always be available.

"Everything's for sale," quipped Serendipity impressario Steven Bruce one recent spring day, as he watered the potted palms. "Well, almost everything." For the past 45 years, Bruce has presided over his beloved restaurant with a combination of showmanship and zealotry.

One item not for sale is the Warhol figurine suspended precariously over the round table that was reserved for the connoisseur of cool. "We hold a séance at this table on Andy's birthday every year," reveals Bruce with a twinkle in his dark eyes. He insists that participants can feel the table tremble. Bruce remembers the artist's final Hot Fudge Sundae, eaten in the company of novelist Tama Janowitz, the night before Andy's hospitalization in 1987, which ended in his death.

Warhol made Serendipity famous for far longer than fifteen minutes—but others loaned it their glamour, too. Marilyn Monroe regularly left lipstick traces on its glassware. On her most famous visit, she arrived wearing a trench coat, kerchief, dark glasses and earrings. She declined to remove the coat, and when asked what she was wearing underneath, she breathily replied, "Chanel #5."

Its register of '50s and '60s movie stars rivals that of C.C. Brown in Hollywood, with Grace Kelly and Jacqueline Onassis also on the list. And the famous keep coming.

Liz Smith revealed that Courtney Love darted outside for a cigarette before finishing her Hot Fudge Sundae. Nicole Kidman created a near riot when she tried to use the ladies room. Julia Roberts quietly played "Clue" with her agent at Serendipity 3.

"Sundaes are ageless, and everyone is open to the experience," philosophizes Bruce. "My guests don't come in for a cup—our Sundaes are dramatic, and theater is the first of all pleasures."

For legions of New Yorkers of a certain age, though, neither the here-and-now spectaculars of Serendipity nor memories or rumors of Rumpelmayer's treats will ever take the place of Sundaes served in Schrafft's.

Opened in 1906, Schrafft's multiplied into fifty-two restaurants before its day was done. Boston hosted six, and Newark, White Plains, Syracuse and Philadelphia each claimed one; the rest were in New York City.

The typical Schrafft's boasted decorous chandeliers, cherry-veneered paneling, upright chairs that encouraged perfect posture and a soda fountain. Even at the fountain, its Sunday goblets were carefully set on lacy paper doilies. Schrafft's leading dessert was the Broadway Sundae, made with chocolate ice cream topped with hot fudge and toasted almonds and pecans.

Schrafft's brought forth lyricism from writers. Poet Phyllis McGinley wrote:

Dear to my heart as to Midas, his coffers,
Are the noontime tables at Schrafft's . . .

A SCHRAFFT'S DINING ROOM STANDING READY FOR THE "MEEK" BUSINESSMEN AND HATTED LADIES WHO LUNCHED THERE.

MORE GIFTS

*I*ce cream can be a soft foundation on which to rest a retail business, particularly in the snow-belt, and especially because Sundaes and related fare are often sold in "family" establishments without liquor licenses. So it is that many emporia also depend on sidelines for their profit.

New Papa Joe's in Flushing, has an unusual merchandise duet: ice cream and plants. You can lap up an old-fashioned Sundae in this Queens malt shop, then carry home a tray of tomato seedlings.

Eddie's Sweet Shop in Forest Hills, once displayed chocolates in its round showcase. Nowadays the antique case holds porcelain dolls and beanie babies. But fine Sundaes still anchor business at this piece of living history, born in 1913. For the last 34 years, the father and son team of Giuseppe and Vito Citrano have been churning out old-fashioned ice creams in the store basement. The ice creams are topped with house-made syrups and freshly-whipped cream piled high in silver-plated goblets. Neighborhood faithful fill the original wooden stools at the marble-topped soda fountain.

Across the city border in Williston Park, Hildebrandt's has been serving egg creams and Sundaes to Long Islanders since 1927. "Everyone here is like family," says Joanne Strano who has presided over the institution since 1974.

For decades, a dentist down the block awarded prescription slips for a "junior Sundae" to be redeemed at Hildebrandt's to youngsters who proved cavity free at check ups. But the sweet prescriptions retired with Dr. Weinstock.

The Hildebrandt Special consists of four scoops of its rich house-made ice cream under the classics—whipped cream, chopped walnuts, cherry—accompanied by a small stainless steel pitcher of hot fudge. And, if that doesn't satisfy one's sweet tooth, rock candy or hand-dipped chocolates are among the gifts that can be purchased at the register.

E. B. White noted, "Businessmen stand in line for a Schrafft's luncheon as meekly as idle men used to stand in soup lines."

In the 1960s, however, most of Schrafft's dwindling clientele appeared be somebody's grandmother or great-aunt. In 1968, the chain so desperately wanted to update its image that it asked Andy Warhol to design a commercial. Warhol's spot opens with a red dot in the darkness,

IF NOT FOR HICKS

*A*nother ice cream parlor in New Yorkers' memories is Hicks. For three-quarters of a century, Hicks did its best to slow down frenzied adults, some accompanied by clamoring children, in its aqua and cotton-candy pink setting. You could order a Supreme Flaming Robin Rose Glowapple, made of orange, pineapple, banana, grapes and strawberries with ice creams of various flavors on top of a slice of pound cake, or you could direct the fountain master to construct a Sundae of your own fantasy. Some Hicks' fans wax rhapsodic over one obliging fountain chief.

Mr. Jennings was beloved by hundreds, possibly thousands of New Yorkers, who would not have dared to ask for his first name. If not for Mr. Jennings, many city children would never have known that dreams and Sundaes are the same thing.

Some of those kids grew up to become patrons of a dim cavern called The Flick. The Flick hired aspiring actresses, dressed them in thigh-high, black net stockings and low-cut leotards, and sent them out to deliver Sundaes with names like Mission Impossible—Burgundy cherry, rum raisin, and eggnog ice creams oozing with butterscotch, marshmallow, hot fudge, crushed pineapple and whipped cream. At 9 p.m., midnight and 3 a.m., the lights went down, and customers were treated to "flicks"—old comedies of W.C. Fields, Laurel and Hardy and Charlie Chaplin.

which lands atop what is revealed as an Ice Cream Sundae, exploding in psychedelic colors.

The voice-over describes this as "Yummy Schrafft's vanilla ice cream in two groovy heaps, with three ounces of mind-blowing chocolate sauce undulating within a mountain of pure whipped cream, topped with a pulsating maraschino cherry, served in a bowl as big as a boat."

The Schrafft's makeover attempt didn't succeed. Its passing from the scene was a drawn-out affair.

Tom Wolfe eulogized the restaurant: "Schrafft's was not exactly the

LAST CHANCE SUNDAE

*W*all Drug, in Wall, South Dakota, may be Serendipity's closest rival in the Campy Sweepstakes. Certainly, Wall Drug did not begin as an exotic enterprise. In 1931, Ted and Dorothy Hustead chose the otherwise unpromising town of Wall for their humble pharmacy and soda fountain because Wall met their two major requirements: It was small but had a Catholic Church.

Wall is on the border of the Badlands.

After five dusty, dry business years, Dorothy, inspired by Burma Shave, had a notion to post "Free Ice Water at Wall Drug" signs for miles out, on all roads leading to, or more frankly around, Wall.

The signs worked. Parched travelers, fearing the wasteland ahead, detoured to Wall Drug. Over the decades, the signs have reached out farther and farther; they now also travel as bumper stickers on seemingly every car that has ever transported tourists to Mt. Rushmore.

Today, Wall Drug is a huge, booming restaurant/showplace, pushing "last-chance" everything—from sustaining Sundaes to a mind-boggling mix of practical paraphernalia and kitschy souveniers. It even has an art gallery.

Wall Drug still sells drugs, including aspirin.

most prestigious place for a woman to eat. But eating at Schrafft's did have a certain secret beauty to it: the much underestimated beauty of American Comfort. The ladies' typical meal at Schrafft's was a cheeseburger, coffee and a Sundae. But such Sundaes! Sundaes with towers of ice cream and nuts and sauces and fudge and maraschino cherries of a quality and buttery beauty such as the outside world has never dreamed of!"

Schrafft's: 1906-1984—may it rest in peace.

THE RECIPES

THE BEST OF SCHRAFFT'S

William Schrafft Schulz of Boston is heir to the Schrafft's legacy by virtue of his great-grandfather's marriage to Louise Schrafft, a daughter of William F. Schrafft, the company founder. Will is the keeper of the original family recipes for Schrafft's butterscotch and hot fudge sauces, which are offered here, with his gracious permission.

You may, however, need more than these two recipes to replicate the pleasure of Sundae eating at genteel Schrafft's. It's recommended that ladies wear hats to the table and that gentlemen help these hat-wearing ladies into their chairs.

HOT FUDGE SAUCE

1 tablespoon unsweetened cocoa powder
1 cup sugar
³/₄ cup heavy cream
¹/₄ cup light corn syrup
2 tablespoons unsalted butter

2 ounces unsweetened chocolate, chopped
1 teaspoon vanilla extract
Pinch of salt
Few drops of malt vinegar

IN A HEAVY MEDIUM SAUCEPAN OVER MEDIUM HEAT, WHISK TOGETHER THE COCOA, SUGAR, AND ¹/₄ CUP OF THE HEAVY CREAM UNTIL SMOOTH, ABOUT 2 MINUTES. STIR IN THE CORN SYRUP, BUTTER, UNSWEETENED CHOCOLATE BITS

AND REMAINING $^1/_2$ HEAVY CREAM, AND BRING TO A BOIL. REMOVE FROM THE HEAT AND STIR IN THE VANILLA, SALT AND VINEGAR.

SAUCE MAY BE REFRIGERATED IN AN AIRTIGHT CONTAINER FOR UP TO 3 WEEKS. TO REHEAT, SET OVER A DOUBLE BOILER, WHISKING VIGOROUSLY. IF RE-HEATING OVER DIRECT HEAT, USE VERY LOW FLAME, AND BE CAREFUL NOT TO LET THE SAUCE BUBBLE OR BURN. MAKES 2 CUPS

BUTTERSCOTCH SAUCE

1 cup packed light brown sugar
$^1/_2$ cup light corn syrup
6 tablespoons ($^3/_4$ stick) unsalt-ed butter

$^1/_8$ tablespoon salt
$^1/_2$ cup heavy cream
$^1/_2$ teaspoon vanilla extract

IN A HEAVY MEDIUM SAUCEPAN, COMBINE THE BROWN SUGAR, CORN SYRUP, BUTTER, AND SALT. BRING TO A BOIL, STIRRING CONSTANTLY, OVER MEDI-UM HEAT, AND COOK FOR ONE MINUTE. TURN OFF THE HEAT AND STIR IN THE CREAM, THEN STIR IN THE VANILLA. ALLOW TO COOL SLIGHTLY (MIXTURE WILL BE VERY HOT). SERVE WARM.

Chapter 17

TRANSATLANTIC CONNECTIONS

*"My advice to you is not to inquire why or whither,
but just enjoy your ice cream while it's on your plate."*
– THORNTON WILDER

Many Americans have viewed traditional French cuisine as enviably scrumptious but also highfalutin' and complex. And the French have thought much American food unsubtle and possibly indigestible, while also being attracted to its modernity. In recent years, *nouvelle cuisine*, with its emphasis on the use of local fresh ingredients in lighter sauces, has enraptured chefs on both sides of the Atlantic and muffled mutual disdain. Nonetheless, envy, naivety and aspiration have left amusing marks on the Sundae world.

Five or more decades ago, when Americans began to embrace "continental" menus, which listed an array of dishes of vaguely European origins as well as American steaks and such, the word *parfait* became attached to a multi-layered Sundae served in an exceptionally tall, fluted glass, accompanied by a long-handled spoon. In French, *parfait* means perfect and many of these Sundaes were and are.

There *is* a French dessert called *parfait*, but it's a semi-frozen mousse. Some restaurateurs were probably under the impression, as many diners came to be, that the parfait was a French creation, and so more luxurious and desirable than even the richest, most painstakingly crafted good old American Sundae.

In the most sophisticated U.S. cities, such as New York and San Francisco, there was custom enough to support authentic French restaurants as well as those of other nationalities. But the parfait not only became a popular dessert in high-priced restaurants in much of the country, it also gained pride of place on the lists of swanky ice cream parlors, decorated in a style meant to suggest Art Nouveau-era Parisian cafés.

Architect G. Morton Wolfe's design for Parkside Candy Company, which opened in 1927 in Buffalo, New York, was inspired by French confectionery salons. Parkside added parfaits to its offerings long ago.

Although the years have not been kind to Parkside's exterior, its extravagant interior oval, domed by a colorful ceiling, has a pleasant fading elegance, perfumed by cocoa butter—the sweet smell of success. Parkside chocolates are displayed like precious jewels in lustrous solid walnut showcases. Parkside Candy also turns out 28,000 lollypops daily (which it wholesales) and spins molasses into sponge candy, a gastronomic triumph almost unknown outside Buffalo.

Although Parkside Candy was conceived in homage to the French, the makers of the movie adaptation of Bernard Malamud's all-American baseball novel, *The Natural* (set in 1936), thought it the quintessential American ice cream parlor and used its interior for a brief scene.

Fountain manager Ann Marie Ranger remembers her first visit to Parkside. "My folks took us to see *The Sound of Music* at the Granada," says Ranger. "Then, after the movie, we walked across the street to Parkside Candy, with everyone still humming *do re mi*."

Ranger's compositional technique in assembling parfaits is so caring that it can only be ascribed to love. She is completely focused as she alternates syrup with egg-shaded French vanilla ice cream in massive Anchor-Hocking goblets for two University of Buffalo seniors.

The results are gorgeous.

The French would recognize Ranger's virtuosity if not her dessert. To anyone interested in the language of food, Parkside's parfaits cross any linguistic barrier.

PERFECT PARFAITS

These are the time-tested parfait rules: Start by putting the syrup or liqueur at the bottom of the glass, use ice cream that has become slightly soft and push down hard every time you add an ice cream layer. This forces the liquid up in the glass, creating the ripple effect that is the signature of a well-made parfait.

TWO VIEWS OF THE PARKSIDE ICE CREAM PARLOR

Some French, however, do recognize the Sundae under its rightful American name. *Le Drugstore* on the Champs Elysées was probably the first Parisian establishment to scoop Hot Fudge Sundaes—and not just for homesick Americans.

At *Berthillon*, on the Ile St. Louis, though, you have to ask for *coup de glace*. Berthillon's ice cream flavors are so intense you can skip the syrup and still have a great time. Scoops are small, as they are in most places on the Continent, so you can eat different flavors at the same time-for instance, *marron* (chestnut) and *poire* (pear).

But the most artistic Sundaes in Paris may be those patrons themselves create at Dammon's. The ice cream balls are placed on a palette-shaped dish with wells filled with different syrups, so you can paint your own combinations.

The classiest Sundae dispensary in Europe is Fortnum and Mason, grocer to the Queen of England. Fortnum boasts four dining rooms, none more fun than The Fountain Restaurant, which proudly serves afternoon ice creams. An old favorite is the Knickerbocker Glory, an ice cream plus crème de menthe concoction that often fits in strawberries, too. The red, green and white Knickerbocker has been knocking around tony English restaurants since the 1930s. "He has the colour sense of a 1950s Knickerbocker Glory," wrote Beatles biographer Philip Norman, describing "Worst Dressed" Richard Whiteley.

Just as many Americans think the parfait is French, some English believe the crème de menthe Sundae to be inherently British. This article of faith is credible, since the defunct, ultra-English Curry's also gloried in the Knickerbocker Glory. The dessert makes its latest literary appearance in J.K. Rowling's *Harry Potter and the Sorcerer's Stone*, when Harry's fat, bratty cousin, Dudley Dursley, complains that his Glory doesn't have enough ice cream on top.

Yet, as any *connoisseur* of American English could tell the Brits, their national Sundae is the namesake of Diedrich Knickerbocker, the eccentric persona Washington Irving created to author his *History of New York*. Knickerbocker was originally the term for a New Yorker of Dutch heritage, although it has come to apply to all New Yorkers.

Hold on to your knickers, here's the kicker: The Knickerbocker Glory is a parfait.

THE RECIPES

PERFECT PARKSIDE PARFAITS
PECAN TURTLE FRAPPÉ

DIP 2 LARGE SCOOPS OF FRENCH VANILLA ICE CREAM INTO A TALL SUNDAE GOBLET. LADLE ON 2 OUNCES OF HOT FUDGE SAUCE AND 2 OUNCES OF HOT CARAMEL SAUCE. GARNISH WITH WHIPPED CREAM, SPRINKLE WITH CHOPPED PECANS, AND PLACE A TURTLE CANDY AT THE TOP.

NOTE: A TURTLE CANDY IS MADE OF VANILLA CARAMEL DEPOSITED OVER A ROASTED PECAN, THEN COVERED IN MILK CHOCOLATE. IF YOU CAN'T FIND A TURTLE, YOU MAY SUBSTITUTE A PECAN.

STRAWBERRY PARFAIT

It's worth shuffling off to Buffalo for this parfait, but I've adapted it here for the home Sundae maker.

Vanilla ice cream
Strawberry Topping (recipe fol-
    lows)

Whipped cream
Maraschino cherries

STRAWBERRY TOPPING

To make the topping, Parkside Candy uses a strawberry concentrate that has been produced by Buffalo jam-makers, Henry and Henry, since 1899. But you can substitute a high-quality supermarket jam. This recipe is enough to top 8 to 10 parfaits.

1 cup strawberry concentrate
1 cup frozen unsweetened straw-
    berries, thawed

1 cup Simple Syrup (recipe follows)
1 teaspoon lemon juice

MIX STRAWBERRIES WITH CONCENTRATE, THEN STIR IN SIMPLE SYRUP AND LEMON JUICE.

SIMPLE SYRUP

1 cup water
1 cup sugar

2 tablespoons light corn syrup

COMBINE WATER, SUGAR AND CORN SYRUP IN A SAUCEPAN AND BRING TO A BOIL, STIRRING UNTIL SUGAR IS DISSOLVED. SIMMER UNDISTURBED FOR 2 MINUTES. COOL TO ROOM TEMPERATURE BEFORE ADDING TO OTHER STRAWBERRY TOPPING INGREDIENTS.

PARFAIT ASSEMBLY

ALTERNATE TOPPING AND ICE CREAM IN A TALL (20-OUNCE) GOBLET. BEGIN BY FILLING A 2-OUNCE LADLE WITH STRAWBERRY TOPPING, AND DROP THE TOPPING TO THE BOTTOM OF THE GLASS. INSERT ONE LARGE SCOOP OF FRENCH VANILLA ICE CREAM, THEN ADD ANOTHER 2 OUNCES OF THE TOPPING. DIP A SECOND LARGE SCOOP OF VANILLA AND ADD 2 MORE OUNCES OF TOPPING. DIP A THIRD SCOOP OF VANILLA AND COVER WITH STRAWBERRY TOPPING. GARNISH WITH WHIPPED CREAM, AND PLACE A MARASCHINO CHERRY ON TOP.

- PARKSIDE CANDY, BUFFALO, NEW YORK

KNICKERBOCKER GLORY

Like any Sundae concept with age to it, the Glory comes with variations. I offer here a slight adaptation of the one served at the late Curry's of London. Curry's topped its creation with a cherry that had been marinated in crème de menthe to great green effect. Food coloring could be used instead, but no harm would be done by sticking to red.

PLACE 2 OUNCES OF CRUSHED STRAWBERRIES AT THE BOTTOM OF A PARFAIT GLASS (TALL SUNDAE GOBLET), FOLLOWED BY A LARGE SCOOP OF VANILLA ICE CREAM. COVER WITH TWO OUNCES OF MARSHMALLOW SYRUP, AND SPRINKLE WITH FINELY CHOPPED HAZELNUTS. THEN ADD 2 OUNCES OF CRUSHED PEACH, CHASED BY A LARGE SCOOP OF STRAWBERRY ICE CREAM. GARNISH WITH WHIPPED CREAM, THEN SPRINKLE WITH FINELY CHOPPED PISTACHIOS. SURMOUNT THE WHOLE WITH A CHERRY.

CRÈME DE MENTHE PARFAIT

The current climate for retro desserts has revived the liqueur and ice cream combination that was on many American restaurant menus in the 1950s, including a legendary outpost on the old route to the Jersey Shore.

PLACE ENOUGH VANILLA OR CHOCOLATE ICE CREAM TO HALF-FILL A SMALL PARFAIT GLASS. ADD CRÈME DE MENTHE, AS DESIRED. FILL REMAINDER OF GLASS WITH ICE CREAM. THE PARFAIT SHOULD BE RETURNED TO THE FREEZER FOR A SHORT TIME TO FIRM UP, THEN GARNISHED WITH WHIPPED CREAM AND MINT LEAVES JUST BEFORE SERVING.

– ELMAROS, MORGAN, NEW JERSEY

Chapter 18

FROM RUSSIA WITH GUILE

*"There's not a thing on earth that I can name
So foolish, and so false as common fame."*

– JOHN WILMOT, EARL OF ROCHESTER (1647-1680)

*P*rince Michael Alexandrovitch Dmitri Obolensky Romanoff, nephew of the last czar, was one of those stories that only happen in Hollywood. He didn't have a drop of royal blood in his veins; he was as phony baloney as they come, but that didn't matter because the people who counted came to his restaurant. "I like Romanoff's because it's the only place to go. I can meet my friends here. It's kind of like a club," Humphrey Bogart explained.

Mike Romanoff, nē Harry Gerguson, served free champagne to the privileged patrons of his Rodeo Drive restaurant. It was domestic, but many of his regulars were either too sloshed or too accustomed to being duped to notice. And he had clout beyond Romanoff's red canopy. Film studios paid him to act as technical advisor on films with Russian locales. The "prince" was a sought-after polo match guest.

Few believed a word he said. In Cold War Hollywood, Mike's acting was fun. "Good afternoon, your royal phoniness," was Bogie's usual greeting.

"Good afternoon, Mr. Bogart," Mike replied in a borrowed Oxford accent. "Are you going to be paying your bill today? I thought that might be a pleasant change."

"Are you going to be putting any alcohol in your overpriced drinks?" Bogart came back.

Romanoff's signature dish was a boozy Ice Cream Sundae. And even that was stolen.

Strawberries Romanoff was the creation of legendary French chef, Auguste Escoffier. Mike passed it off as a family heirloom when he introduced it at his tables in 1941. Within three months, the flamboyant ice

MIKE ROMANOFF WAS A PHONY PRINCE WITH AN AUTHENTICALLY GLORIOUS (IF STOLEN) SUNDAE RECIPE.

© CORBIS/BETTMAN

cream dessert with orange liqueur-flavored strawberries topped with sweetened whipped cream was replicated in ritzy restaurants throughout California. Numerous interpretations now exist. James Beard wrote, "If there is one satisfactory version of Strawberries Romanoff, there are twenty-five."

Romanoff's world was endearing, just not enduring. The joint went kaput in 1962, much to the distress of director Billy Wilder, who grumbled, "There are more bad restaurants in L.A. than bad film directors." Wilder convinced fifty friends to invest $3,000 each in a replacement he dubbed The Bistro. He put Romanoff's maitre d', Kurt Niklas, in charge, who hired unemployed Romanoff waiters. They even served the royal Strawberry Sundae. But without a fake Russian prince to rule, the gloss was gone, and the ersatz Romanoff's had only a short run.

THE RECIPES

STRAWBERRIES ROMANOFF

Jug-eared Mike Romanoff stood just five-feet-five inches tall, perpetually dressed in flamboyant jackets, and sported a pencil-thin moustache and military-style crew cut. The only truism at Romanoff's was that anyone who knew anything about food saved room for this dessert. This recipe serves 4.

1 pint choice strawberries	*1 cup whipped cream*
3 ounces Cointreau	*1 pint vanilla ice cream*

MARINATE STRAWBERRIES IN THE LIQUEUR UNDER REFRIGERATION FOR 1 HOUR. AT THE TABLE, ARRANGE 3 BOWLS, EACH SET IN A BED OF ICE: ONE BOWL OF WHIPPED CREAM, ONE OF ICE CREAM AND ONE OF STRAWBERRIES. COMBINE INGREDIENTS FOR EACH GUEST.

Chapter 19

MOTHER OF ALL SUNDAES

"Nothing succeeds like excess."

– OSCAR WILDE

The jam-packed Ice Cream Sundae is a metaphor for American big-ness and indulgence. We have more of most good things than most other places, and there are practically no bounds to size in either the portions at our tables or in other exaggerations in our national life. As *New York Times* columnist Maureen Dowd once wrote, "We don't have limits. We have liberties . . . We are America."

That doesn't mean that Americans won't accept curtailment of pleasures in times of crisis. We've accepted sacrifices, including culinary ones, since colonial patriots dumped tea in Boston harbor. Nonetheless, Americans, by nature and fortunate circumstance, are generous; we are not stingy with others, and unnecessary self-denial is not part of our national character, either.

In some ways, our national propensities were foreshadowed by the 18th-century patriot and Revolutionary general, Israel Putnam. Old Put's personal indulgence was cigars (which he went to great length to obtain), not ice cream, which was then known only in circles more cos-mopolitan than his. He was a courageous, colorful individual whose biggest

A TASTE OF TWAIN

"We do not get ice cream everywhere, and so, when we do, we are apt to dissipate to excess." – MARK TWAIN, *INNOCENTS ABROAD*

REVOLUTIONARY HERO ISRAEL PUTNAM'S BIRTHPLACE HOUSES THE FIRST SUNDAE SMORGASBROD.

appetite was for liberty, and although it may be coincidental, it's fitting that his descendant runs a Sundae extravaganza in his very birthplace.

Putnam was born in Salem Village, Massachusetts; the town is now called Danvers.

As soon as Putnam received word of the "shots heard 'round the world," those igniting the skirmishes at Concord and Lexington, he dropped his plow, unyoked his team and rode off to join the battle, without so much as a change of clothes.

Two months later, he led a brigade at Bunker Hill. As a swarm of British advanced in their scarlet coats, Putnam had his men lie in wait to attack until the last possible second, since they held precious little ammunition. He issued the now-famous command, "Men, you are all marksmen-don't one of you fire until you see the whites of their eyes!" Then, with a deafening roar amid plumes of gunpowder smoke, the ragtag colonials drove back the British.

At first glance, 21st-century Danvers lacks outward charm. It sits beside the great highway, U.S.1 (which runs from the top of Maine to the Florida Keys), but it is perfectly possible to pass by Danvers without being tempted to stop. For a history lover or a Sundae lover, that would be a mistake.

Perched on the cloverleaf just off Rte.1 is the house built by General Putnam's grandfather, still owned by the Putnam family. And the original Putnam homestead built just 28 years after the Pilgrims dis-

A BILLION COOKIES, ANYONE?

In theory, at least, if every Oreo cookie ever made (350 billion) were placed in one stack, the pile would reach to the moon and back more than five times. You can make your own Sundae out of what has been America's leading cookie since it was introduced in 1912. The Leaning Tower of Oreos Sundae, promoted by the folks at Nabisco, uses chocolate fudge swirl ice cream as cement between as many Oreos as you can pile up. Drizzle the stack with fudge sauce and finish with whipped cream.

embarked from the Mayflower is now a candy factory and ice cream parlor. An historical marker announces you are in the right place when you drive up to the clapboard saltbox housing Putnam Pantry.

Ten generations removed from "Old Put," Galo Putnam Emerson became a folk hero to ice cream lovers when he invented the Ice Cream Sundae bar, back in 1958. Emerson is the proprietor and head confectioner of Putnam Pantry, started by his father.

As a child, Galo would linger for hours, watching the candy and ice cream makers apply their trades. He thought it would be fun to spend his days stirring and tasting sweet treats, but his father had a different notion of Galo's future. Galo Putnam Emerson went off to Harvard where he prepared for a career in finance. Nonetheless, when his father retired, Galo was delighted to take charge of the business.

On an early morning, one can find Galo Emerson downstairs, attired in comfortable Boston tweeds, surrounded by elaborate candy-making equipment. Emerson is the chief candy-maker, and he has about three hundred varieties in his repertoire. His calling does not tire him. "It's the most relaxing part of my day," he says. He arranges seventy pecan patties on a large tray; by hand he drops dots of caramel on the pecans. Next, a machine enrobes the patties with milk chocolate. The result: melt-in-your-mouth candies.

Charm exudes from all directions in cheerful Putnam Pantry: Display cases and tables are laden with so many delicious-looking candies that it's hard to make a pick. A hodgepodge of Colonial furniture, knickknacks and vintage soda fountain furniture make its rooms inviting. Above one fireplace is a portrait of Gen. Putnam.

Yet the heart of the enterprise is the Ice Cream Smorgasbord, a name to which Putnam Pantry holds a copyright. "It's hard to impress New Englanders with ice cream," Emerson says. "Back in the 1950s, we thought it would be a clever idea to let customers make their own Sundaes. We served a goblet of ice cream, then brought a Lazy Susan over to the table. It contained half a dozen bowls filled with toppings. Needless to say, it was a huge mess and a complete disaster. It wasn't until we built a self-service buffet table that the idea actually worked."

In fact, it worked so well, eager customers waited in long lines for the privilege of attacking the Ice Cream Smorgasbord. Think of the 14-foot stainless steel Sundae bar as the anti-salad bar. Instead of loading up on one or two varieties of tasteless, tired lettuce and the kind of disease-resistant tomatoes that *Newsday* writer Mike McGrady once described as "baseballs in drag," the customer gets to cruise past sixteen flavors of ice cream and three frozen yogurts. The color orange comes not in the form of iced carrots but as orange sherbet.

The moment of truth arrives as soon as you hit the Sundae bar. You need to choose a silver-colored bowl to begin: Will it be the junior size, the regular, or large?

RECORD HOLDERS

Each year the folks in Burlington, Washington, build an insulated foam dish, eight feet long, four feet high, and four feet wide, and place it in the center of town to hold the "largest" Sundae in the world, from which hundreds of people are served. But apparently this happy effort is not big enough to satisfy the "Guinness Book of World Records".

The Guinness blue-ribbon Sundae was created in Anaheim, California, in 1985. That Sundae weighed in at 27,102 pounds, with 4,667 gallons of ice cream piled 12 feet high, dripping with 7,000 pounds of topping!

A server scoops in your choices of ice cream/frozen yogurt/sherbet. Now you must decide whether to ladle on hot fudge, hot butterscotch, hot penuche (brown sugar fudge sauce) or dark chocolate sauce-or maybe some of each. Regulars know that each of Emerson's toppings is really special, so this is not an easy call.

Then, what will it be? Sliced strawberries, crushed pineapple, or shredded coconut? Chopped walnuts and/or peanuts? Macaroon crunch or crushed Oreos? Whipped cream or marshmallow syrup? A sprinkle of jimmies or not?

You can wait until you see the smoothness of the sauces or the whites of the coconuts and marshmallows (to paraphrase Emerson's ancestor) before you decide what to shoot into your bowl, but there is no room for miscalculation, as only one pass-through is allowed. On the other hand, it's pretty tough to make a serious error: this is your vision of all a Sundae can be. My advice, should you decide to lay siege to the Ice Cream Smorgasbord is: Throw caution to the wind, but don't forget the cherry on top.

It's also great fun to watch and listen in on some of the Smorgasbord patrons, particularly the newcomers who don't yet get the rules. On my last visit, the enthusiasm of a group of five giggling, age thirty-something girlfriends was truly inspirational. The first in line quizzed the ice cream server. "Is it all you can eat? Can you go up six times?"

"I need this like I need a hole in the head!" declared the second, as she loaded strawberries and hot fudge atop the high-butterfat vanilla in her large-size bowl. She then piled the whipped cream so high that when she added the cherry it started to sway in the goo.

SUNDAE SATIRE?

In a 1971 commercial, adman Stan Freberg described a mountain of whipped cream on Lake Michigan onto which the Air Force dropped a 10-ton cherry, touting radio's power to "stretch the imagination." Was the notion of Lake Michigan as a Sundae bowl a mockery of American gullibility and appetite? I'd say it was a celebration of both.

SUNDAE, SCHMUNDAE

*F*irst in the hearts and stomachs of those who've ventured into a Jahn's ice cream parlor in the New York area or, eventually, Miami Beach, is the masterwork called The Kitchen Sink, made of "everything else but." The last open Jahn's branch in Richmond Hills, Queens, still offers this seventeen-scoop creation—at $38.65.

Since 1990, Kiev emigrants Igor and Alla Mikit have owned this Jahn's, running it in the tradition of working seven days a week—just like the founder, German immigrant John Jahn, ran his Bronx store. Old menus told the story:

"The year is 1888—winter—snowing to beat all ice cream. A sailing vessel makes port at New York and who steps off but John Jahn, age 14, hereafter called Papa. A real greenhorn with nothing but ambition. Five years of working at a bakery at ten dollars per month with board. Papa didn't go too much for the heat, having come from a cold country, so he got a job as an ice cream maker for a store in Brooklyn. He froze along and finally met Mama, at a dancing school called Weber's. A married man has to be able to support a family so Papa opened his first store in the Bronx at 138th Street and Alexander Avenue in 1897...ice cream sold for twenty-cents a quart, which was never measured but just tossed into whatever can or dish you brought... Along came Elsie, then Frank and finally Howard. Papa finally decided to take a rest in 1918. He vacationed for about five years and then decided there was no reason his children shouldn't go into the same business, so he opened a store for Elsie in Jamaica, a store for Frank in Richmond Hill and a store for Howard in Flushing."

"Sundaes, Mondaes, Shmundaes," read the advertisements for the Sundaes of Jahn's children. "What's the difference? Try one and see." Besides the Kitchen Sink, customers, serenaded by Nickelodean melodies, ate concoctions such as Miami Mish Mash and Screwball's Delight ("drive you nuts and plenty of them").

The Mikits serve some familiar Jahn's Sundaes plus new ones, for instance the Super Candy Sundae which incorporates rocky road ice cream, chocolate syrup, whipped cream, M & Ms and rainbow sprinkles under a red cherry.

MENU

JAHN'S

SINCE 1897

OLD FASHIONED
ICE CREAM PARLOR
AND
RESTAURANT

andrew g fischer

17262 COLLINS AVENUE
MIAMI BEACH, FLORIDA
Tel. DAde 6-9342

MENU FROM THE NOW-GONE MIAMI OUTPOST OF JAHN'S.

Another of the young women chose her toppings with extreme care, accessorizing her ice cream in color-balanced combinations.

The Sundae bar brings out a little gluttony in almost everyone, Emerson has observed. "People really pile on the toppings," he notes, "so we give them a plate underneath to catch whatever falls off."

Putnam Pantry also offers the opportunity to make your own banana split.

Its best deal, however, is the preposterous-sized Sundae, called "Battle of Bunker Hill." This seventeen-scoop platter of Americana sells for $17.76, and is a favorite of high school soccer and baseball teams.

"It has always been seventeen scoops, it has always been priced at $17.76—and it always will be," laments Emerson. "It pays no attention to inflation. It's an historical imperative."

God bless the Putnam Pantry.

THE RECIPES

WHEELBARROW SUNDAE

*I*mpressive as the Battle of Bunker Hill Sundae is, and it is impressive, being the biggest of anything takes place on a battlefield whose lines are constantly extended. Not only are there one-time or even annual feats that outdo the Bunker Hill, there are establishments that regularly do special Sundaes for crowds. And some of these party-menu Sundaes are bigger than Putnam Pantry's homage to the American Revolution. But wouldn't you know it? The biggest Sundae I've come across is served on territory that Gen. Putnam once marshaled.

• •

DIP 200 LARGE SCOOPS OF ICE CREAM INTO A FOIL-LINED, FULL-SIZE WHEELBARROW. TOP WITH $1/2$ GALLON EACH OF CHOCOLATE SYRUP AND CRUSHED STRAWBERRIES. PEEL AND SPLIT ONE LARGE BUNCH OF BANANAS AND PLACE AROUND THE BASE OF THE ICE CREAM. GARNISH WITH $1/2$ GALLON OF WHIPPED HEAVY CREAM, AND PLACE ONE PINT OF MARASCHINO CHERRIES AT THE TOP.

• •

– MORTENSEN'S, NEWINGTON, CONNECTICUT

Chapter 20

LOVIN' SPOONFULS

"What the Contract [with America] says is that you can have a Hot Fudge Sundae with every meal and still lose weight."

—WALL STREET JOURNAL EDITOR AL HUNT

The American food pyramid, diagramming everything we *should* eat, looks suspiciously like an Ice Cream Sundae. Sundaes, any way you scoop them, are beloved; yet at any given time of year, one-third of us are trying to shed pounds.

This contradiction prompted the novel idea of Rosy and Rich Bergin, who have conspired against culinary dogma to create a dessert contained in a single piece of tableware. Think small. That's what they do at the *Shark and Rose, a cozy restaurant and pub in San Jose, California, where a bastion of foodies have embraced the itsy-bitsy inspiration called Soup Spoon Sundae.

Once upon a time, when many of us believed Sundaes were a daily right, the pressure our culture places on women to fit into smaller-size dresses provoked a "balanced" ladylike meal: salad, diet drink, and a Hot Fudge Sundae. Now many would scoff at the discipline in that, but we are still left trying to stay or become thin, while pacifying our demanding sweet tooth.

"My customers can't say 'no' to a dessert this size, no matter how full they are after dinner," Rosy Bergin explains. "It's just one spoonful!"

This dessert is never shared. A little of what you fancy does you good, it is said, but how many of us can stop after just a little ice cream? Apparently, many Shark and Rose patrons can. Still, there are a few who order second helpings of the splendid little Sundae with the wincingly cute name.

Rosy Bergin reminds some people of Martha Stewart. The comparison holds up if you can picture Martha spiking a volleyball between turns of sparkling cooking and decorative upkeep. Rosy, who stands nearly six feet tall, is a veteran of five years on the Women's Professional Beach Volleyball tour. She is still constantly on the run, sharing management responsibilities for three restaurants with her husband and business partner, Rich Bergin.

Rich is an Irish version of John Travolta, athletic and perennially boyish-looking. The Soup Spoon Sundae was his brainstorm.

In 1996, when the couple was getting ready to open their second restaurant, they settled easily on the name, Shark and Rose. "Dock shark" was the nickname local fishermen had given to Rich after his first venture had made him a ready customer for half the fresh catch at Half Moon Bay. "Rose," of course, is his wife's proper name.

Rich and Rosy liked the *Cheers* theme song, which marked the TV-show hangout as a place "where everybody knows your name." They figured that the exposed brick and mahogany finishes already in place in their new space (a British-type pub in its previous incarnation) would set the Cheer-ful tone for the conviviality they wanted.

They planned to repeat the successful seafood entrees of their first restaurant plus offer interesting new dishes like Fish Tacos—grilled salmon, swordfish or shark served on soft corn tortillas with avocado and cole slaw.

But what about desserts? Here they hoped to be original, but figuring out their dessert carte held a special challenge. "I thought we'd spotted a dangerous trend in the first restaurant, as dessert sales

IT COULD'VE BEEN A CONTENDER

Chicago's lavish, old-line Pump Room long claimed the World's Smallest Hot Fudge Sundae. This Sundae was served to the likes of industrialists, star architects and visiting theatrical personalities, comfortably ensconced in massive banquette seats under glittering chandeliers and blue and gold fabric streamers. The World's Smallest Hot Fudge Sundae, more often than not, followed a very large steak. In 1998, an over-zealous new chef threw the legendary Sundae off the Pump Room menu.

ANOTHER TITLE CLAIMANT

Ed Debevic stepped into the ring to keep small Sundaes in Chicago, introducing them in his eponymous diner-themed eateries. His tiny Hot Fudge starts with a one-ounce scoop of vanilla. The finished Sundae comes to a customer in an ornate, eye-wash-cup-size, sherry-glass-shaped goblet, accompanied by a tiny spoon. The cunning little glass is emblazoned with Ed Debevic's logo. Once customers have downed the Sundae in a swallow or two, they're welcome to take the goblet home as a souvenir.

gave way to more conscientious dieting," says Rich. "When desserts become bigger and bigger, it gets easier to pass on them entirely. After all, for most of us, the hard truth is that the only way to stay slim is to eat less."

While the Soup Spoon Sundae may have been Rich's bright idea, it was left to Rosy to figure out how to put it together. "It was a pain in the neck," Rosy says. "No one could find a commercial dipper small enough." She experimented until she found that a restaurant bouillon spoon would work. Rosy then slaved some more to get the little devil just right.

The perfect solution also rested on the ice cream-scooping technique Rosy had learned when she was fifteen and working at a local ice cream shop. To make the Soup Spoon Sundae, she rolled the bouillon spoons across the inside of a tub of vanilla ice cream. A seamless motion allowed for a bit of air in the middle, as she got a strip of ice cream to curl around itself until she had formed a scoop that fit neatly in the spoon's shallow bowl.

Rose decided to keep the perfect mini-scoop in the spoon, so she drizzled on chocolate and then dabbed a very restrained dollop of whipped cream on top.

The spoon would be placed on a clean white plate for service.

Craig Claiborne once observed, "I have learned that nothing can equal the universal appeal of the food of one's childhood and early youth."

The truth of his remark is affirmed as a Shark and Rose server holds aloft a tray of Soup Spoon Sundaes intended for a party of six grown-ups. As the waitress zeroes in on the target table, diners at other tables in the busy room take note. When she presents the diminutive desserts, all six spoons on a single oyster plate, everyone at the table breaks into applause.

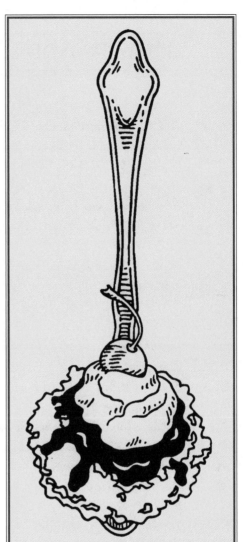

The server gives each diner a small dessert plate. As she circles the table, presenting the Sundae platter to each diner, a tanned blonde, the paradigm of thin, looks absolutely giddy. But the fellow next to her appears slightly discomfited. He must be thinking: *Is that all there is?*

There is a pause when each dessert eater has his or her spoon by the handle. Two customers stare at their desserts for a second, then at each other, perhaps considering proper etiquette. Emily Post never thought of this one. Left on their own, half of the six choose to nibble around the spoon. The other three decide to help it off the spoon and onto the plate–the preferred method, according to the Bergins.

There is something quite heartening as well as amusing in this smaller-than-life Sundae saga. "Some of our customers see the difference of an ounce or two as a real moral choice," explains Rosy.

In America you can have your Sundae and feel virtuous about it, too.

How to Add Calories to Yogurt

*F*rank D. Hickingbotham hated yogurt, until his wife got him to try the Daniel Brackeen's frozen yogurt sold at Neiman Marcus in Dallas. After his first bite he exclaimed, "This can't be yogurt!"

The result was Hickingbotham's store, This Can't Be Yogurt, in the Market Place shopping center in Little Rock, Arkansas. Twenty years later, ICBY (which now stands for The Country's Best Yogurt) has 3,000 locations in the United States and abroad.

ICBY Enterprises reports its most-requested toppings are:

1. Hot Fudge
2. Strawberries
3. Non-fat Hot Fudge
4. Walnuts in Syrup
5. Chocolate Chip Cookie Dough
6. M&Ms Plain Chocolate Candies
7. Hot Cherry Topping
8. Oreo Cookies
9. Hot Caramel
10. Gummy Bear Candies

Chapter 21

SUNDAE HEAVEN

"I do not approve of mourning, I approve only of remembering."

– NOEL COWARD

ooth Five, the L-shaped, gold-vinyl seat in the corner of a beloved Chicago sweet shop, is where George Poulos proposed to Margie Michaels in 1932.

Depending on your point of view, the shop is either cluttered and cramped or intimate and romantic but, in either case, it's where this love story begins. She was a carpenter's pretty daughter, hired to work at Security Candies; almost as soon as she said "yes" to the proposal, the name of the store was changed to Margie's.

Downtown Chicago is architecturally adventurous, yet its neighborhoods resist change. One happy consequence is that when it comes to ice cream locales, more than a few of the genuine articles survive. The ice cream shop that became Margie's Candies has stood like a rock in Bucktown since George Poulos's father opened it for business in 1921. Margie's is actually a combination of restaurant, ice cream parlor, candy shop, and toy store—a tiny place, only slightly more commodious than a phone booth, with a big, nourishing tradition.

There is nothing about the unassuming storefront that might tip a casual passer-by to the fact that he or she has found the single best place for Ice Cream Sundaes in the city. But stop and ask someone on line what he or she is waiting for. Whatever the time, stop inside and pick up a menu, choose from 2-dip to 25-dip concoctions, and—oh, Lord!— you'll know this is Sundae Heaven.

Shelves are tightly filled with chocolates, porcelain dolls, stuffed animals, knickknacks, and goodness knows what else. Strains of sentimentality may be ordered up for a quarter at tabletop consolette juke-boxes. Truffles and turtles cool on marble slabs behind the counter. For much of the ice cream store's life, its greatest distinction was Margie herself, according to her son, Peter Poulos, inheritor of Margie's and keeper of its faith.

In her younger days, Margie Poulos labored as a candy dipper in the early morning, then as a waitress when the store opened. Standing just over five feet tall, she wore a floral-print dress covered with a starched white apron every day. And she braided and pinned up her long, glorious hair so it would not interfere with work. Margie was very proud that the store carried her name, and she worked tirelessly to make it better.

Then came World War II. George left to defend the country, and Margie was left to defend the store. Not only did she come up with deft Sundaes despite sugar rationing and chocolate shortages, she took night classes at a business school. One time Margie took the train to New York to attend candy-making classes. She also managed during the war years to remodel the shop.

When the war ended, George returned home to find that sales had doubled.

Margie made her own ice cream and was not willing to compromise her handcrafted product with ordinary fixings, so she made the Sundae toppings, too. "There's nothing complicated about making a really good Sundae," she would say. "All you need is the very best ice cream and the highest quality toppings."

There are no wimpy Sundaes at Margie's. The Ice Cream Sundaes are served in huge, white plastic shells. You need to think twice before ordering a meal—this is the kind of place where a Hot Fudge Sundae is dinner. An enormous portion of ice cream is accompanied by a stainless-steel urn of rich, deep, dark, bittersweet hot fudge sauce.

How can anything compare to the likes of the Jumbo Fudge Atomic Sundae? The customer's choice of ice cream is covered by a lattice of candy-dipping chocolate, which hardens just as it hits the ice cream. This marvelous beauty then disappears under an enormous cloud of whipped cream and chopped nuts, with a cherry dotting its top. The Atomic Sundae is presented on a silver platter with a lace doily, and served with the fudge-filled urn and bright yellow vanilla wafers.

Little about Margie's Candies has changed since Margie exchanged the heaven-on-earth she had created for the big Sundae parlor above.

Peter Poulos, who introduces himself as "Margie's son," is happy to tell stories of the past. Like other children of remarkable ice cream makers, he grew up in the candy store, but the thought was he'd do something else in his maturity. For Peter, the something else was following his

MARGIE'S CANDIES ON A SUMMER DAY.

mother's advice and becoming a podiatrist. But even while Peter Poulos was tending to his patients' sore feet, he was linked to Margie's. More than once, he postponed a patient appointment so he could run an errand for Mom.

Just before Easter in 1995, Margie, still going strong, spent a whole day tying bows to candy baskets. The next day she passed away at age 80. In short order, Peter Poulos retired from his practice to keep Margie's Candies alive.

"The experience is not just about the candy and ice cream, but about the whole magical world of it," says Poulos. "All the ingredients of life are here."

A place like Margie's was hardly a neighborhood secret, even in the days when Sundaes were served on almost every street.

Walt Disney celebrated a birthday here. The Beatles sneaked into Margie's after their 1965 concert in Comiskey Park. After eating his Sundae, John Lennon danced with Margie to music from the consolette. Sundae seekers transcend categories. Margie's Sundaes have been served up to Michael Jackson, Meryl Streep and Rev. Billy Graham.

TORONTO
TERRIFIC

Some of the best ice creams in North America are in Canada, and in Toronto there's one Sundae maker who produces almost unearthly Sundaes from ice creams he makes himself. Gary Stephen Theodore has been upstaging many of his counterparts to the south ever since he opened the first Caffé Demetré in 1989.

Theodore traces his roots to a Greek-immigrant ancestor who operated the Yorkville Candy Kitchen in York, South Carolina, back in the early 1900s. Three generations later, Theodore is making ice creams whose richness and flavor might have impressed his great grandfather even if their names were unfamiliar. Theodore's high-concept ice cream parlors now number ten locations in greater Toronto.

"Ice cream is the easiest food to glamorize," says the energetic Theodore, who supplemented family traditions by attending Penn State's prestigious Ice Cream Science program. His passionate approach for Caffé Demetré has produced Sundaes on top of French Toast, Sundaes on top of Belgian Waffles, and Sundaes inside French crepes. Among the masterpieces on his long, creative menu is the Freudian Dip: One scoop of Chocolatta, a rich chocolate ice cream, rolled in white chocolate chunks, and one scoop of Belgian White Chocolate ice cream rolled in dark chocolate chunks, served on a bed of triple fudge sauce topped with more triple fudge.

Nonetheless, it's the regulars who keep Margie's throbbing year after year. "It kind of gives me goose bumps to walk in here," says Zenaida Lopez, who owns a nearby Puerto Rican bakery. She had her first Margie's Sundae one afternoon after high school band practice—thirty five years ago—and has been a loyal customer ever since.

"Margie was a beautiful woman who aged gracefully," remembers Ms. Lopez while feasting on her usual midday Hot Fudge Sundae. "She sat at the cash register and took the money, and at the same time directed her staff like a traffic cop." The tip of Ms. Lopez's spoon produces a scraping sound as she finishes the last bit of hot fudge clinging to the bottom of her Sundae dish. "Ahhh," she says, a satisfied look settling on her face, "just like it ever was."

Margie is the patron saint of Ice Cream in Chicago. She dedicated her life to the store that bears her name, and the city is richer for it.

THE RECIPES

MARGIE'S MAGIC

You don't have to serve these Sundaes in quirky plastic shells as Margie's does. But you'll need to use large dishes and create or buy the very best ingredients you can to even begin to approximate the generosity of Margie Poulos's Sundaes.

BUCKTOWN SPECIAL

DIP 2 LARGE SCOOPS OF VANILLA ICE CREAM INTO A WIDE SHELL. SURROUND THE ICE CREAM WITH ROUND SLICES OF BANANA, THEN COVER WITH HOT FUDGE SAUCE AND MARSHMALLOW SYRUP GARNISH WITH WHIPPED CREAM, AND PLACE A MARASCHINO CHERRY AT THE TOP. TWO VANILLA WAFERS COME ON THE SIDE.

PINA COLADA SUNDAE

DIP 4 LARGE SCOOPS OF VANILLA ICE CREAM INTO A WIDE SHELL. SURROUND THE ICE CREAM WITH ROUND SLICES OF BANANA AND BITE-SIZE CHUNKS OF FRESH PINEAPPLE. GARNISH WITH WHIPPED CREAM, AND PLACE A MARASCHINO AT THE TOP. SERVE WITH AN URN OF HOT FUDGE SAUCE AND 2 VANILLA WAFERS.

ROYAL GEORGE
SUNDAE

*T*his one is a party special, named after Margie's husband. You'll have to use your imagination to find a big-enough dish; a large punch bowl might work.

DIP 25 LARGE SCOOPS OF VANILLA ICE CREAM (OR YOUR CHOICE OF FLA-VOR—PLENTY OF ROOM HERE TO MIX SEVERAL) INTO AN OVERSIZED SHELL. SURROUND THE ICE CREAM WITH WAFFLE CONES, UPSIDE-DOWN TO FORM A CROWN FOR "ROYAL GEORGE," AND LOAD ON THE WHIPPED CREAM. ACCOMPANY WITH A TRAY OF HOT-FUDGE PITCHERS AND SIX BOWLS, EACH FILLED WITH A DIF-FERENT FAVORITE GARNISH.

– MARGIE'S CANDIES, CHICAGO, ILLINOIS

MERRY-GO-ROUND SUNDAE

What goes round comes round in the Chicago suburb of Oak Park. In 1931, Danish immigrant Hans Petersen moved his ice cream shop to Chicago Avenue (in what's known as the Frank Lloyd Wright historical district), and it has been serving whimsical Sundaes at the same location ever since. Petersen appreciated loyalty; his will, executed in 1963, left his establishment to five employees, who had been with him at least thirty years. Their heirs sold the shop in 1974. Fortunately, its current owners appreciate its traditions.

· ·

DIP ONE LARGE SCOOP OF VANILLA ICE CREAM ONTO THE CENTER OF A FLAT SUNDAE DISH. COVER THE ICE CREAM WITH CHOCOLATE SYRUP AND STICK A PAPER UMBRELLA IN THE TOP. SURROUND WITH ANIMAL CRACKERS FOR THE RIDE.

· ·

– PETERSEN'S OLD-FASHIONED ICE CREAMS, OAK PARK, ILLINOIS

MUDDLE SUNDAE

At age nine, James Papageorge was a successful transatlantic stowaway who then made his way to Chicago, where he found work as a soda jerk. Papageorge saved his pennies, and in 1920 he bought the ice cream parlor nestled next to the Gayety Theater on Chicago's South Side. The theater is long gone, but Gayety's Chocolates and Ice Cream still thrives in the hands of the Papageorge family.

· ·

DIP ONE LARGE SCOOP OF VANILLA-BEAN ICE CREAM INTO A SUNDAE TULIP. COVER THE ICE CREAM WITH CARAMEL SAUCE. GARNISH WITH WHIPPED CREAM AND SPRINKLE WITH WHOLE ROASTED PECANS. SERVE WITH A SMALL PITCHER OF HOT FUDGE SAUCE.

· ·

– GAYETY'S CHOCOLATES AND ICE CREAM COMPANY, CHICAGO, ILLINOIS

Chapter 22

SONGBIRD SUNDAES

"She was a Butterscotch Sundae of a woman."

– A. J. LIEBLING

The woman in question was Lillian Russell, a much-admired song-bird in the early years of the 20th century. And her beauty was well matched by the words that flowed from A.J. Liebling, who was a food fancier (preferring simple food), a woman fancier (at least in his prose) and a life fancier extraordinaire. Liebling continued, " If a Western millionaire, one of the Hearst or Mackay kind, could have given an architect a carte blanche to design a woman, she would have looked like Lillian. She was San Simeon in corsets."

Lillian Russell required corsets, not only because it was her misfortune to be a lady in an era where fashionable woman sucked it in with a hoopla of string pulling and help from strong stays, but also because she was lusciously *ample*—in the way that worldly woman use to be, which was also the way that men who loved them wanted them to be.

Lillian worked—although it may have been enjoyable labor—at being a woman of full measure by eating a fourteen-course dinner every night,

---

TOO HAUGHTY FOR SUNDAES

In the recent period-piece film, *"Tea with Mussolini"*, Maggie Smith portrays Lady Hester Random, a quintessential English snob. Anything that doesn't conform to her notion of propriety becomes subject to her scorn. Observing an Ice Cream Sundae being served, she sniffs that Americans have even found a way to *"vulgarize ice cream."*

culminating with an ice cream dessert. The Waldorf Astoria named her favorite combination after her. The "Lillian Russell" memorialized ice cream scooped into a half cantaloupe.

In retrospect, we'd probably call Australian diva Nellie Melba "a peach of a woman," so attached has her last name become to vanilla ice cream matched with poached peaches in a raspberry swirl. But before Nellie was a Sundae, she was a popular coloratura soprano, adored by Gay Nineties critics and fans. George Bernard Shaw wrote that Melba at her best sang with a "superhuman beauty." Tenor Jean de Reszke said she had a

LILLIAN RUSSEL.

"voice of gold, the most beautiful of our time." Sarah Bernhardt thought it a "voice of pure crystal."

Nellie attributed her success to her perfectionism. Hearing another rave review, she'd shrug and say, "If I'd been a maid, I'd have been the best maid in Australia. It's got to be perfection for me." She often happily declared, "I'm a damned snob!" Those who knew her best agreed.

Melba, however, did worry that she might weigh a bit too much to cut a perfect figure. Her favorite reducing exercise was rolling back and forth on the floor, which she'd do impulsively, even in a Parisian silk gown.

Inevitably, Dame Nellie's sparkling path crossed that of another perfectionist. Her equal in artistry was the French chef Auguste Escoffier, who brilliantly ruled over the kitchen and tables of London's Savoy Hotel. Escoffier's passions extended beyond the Savoy to the Royal Opera House at Covent Garden, where he, too, worshiped Nellie Melba, who often dined at the Savoy. One spring evening in 1893, he attended a production of Wagner's *Lohengrin*. Nellie's enchanting performance as Elsa put a lump in his throat.

He determined to thank her by creating a dish that would perfectly commemorate the occasion.

The next day, Melba arrived for luncheon, carrying her enamel-handled umbrella studded with tiny diamond flowers and gold leaves. She ordered the plover's eggs *en croute* with fresh caviar, and washed it down with champagne.

When it came time for dessert, Escoffier entered the dining room carrying a silver bowl bearing a carved ice swan—inspired by the majestic swan of *Lohengrin's* first act. A poached half peach, filled with ice cream, was tucked under each big wing of the swan and netted in lacy spun sugar. The dessert must have tasted as good as it looked, because Dame Nellie ate every bite.

Escoffier served subsequent Peach Melbas with a swan whose wings were made of edible meringue. Years later, at the opening of the Carlton Hotel in London, he decided to improve upon the Melba with the addition of a purée of raspberries and a sprinkling of shredded green almonds.

Escoffier was insightful and direct when it came to preparation and presentation of food. He was quick to praise great dishes of other chefs, but equally quick to chastise them for what he considered miscalculations. And nothing irked him more than the liberties others took in reinterpreting Peach Melba, replacing the raspberry purée with strawberry jam or currant jelly, or decorating the peaches with whipped cream. "The results obtained," he insisted, "have absolutely nothing to do with the original recipe and could hardly satisfy the palate of a real connoisseur."

A *New York Times* reporter, woefully ignorant of the history of ice cream delights, drew the task of writing Escoffier's obituary in 1935. In it was the outlandish suggestion that Peach Melba had inspired the American Sundae.

I would not go so far as to suggest that it was vice versa. Escoffier was a man gifted enough to come up with majestic Sundaes on his own; you will recall that he was also the rightful creator of Strawberries Romanoff, purloined by a royal impostor. He also created Cherries Jubilee.

Arguably, the Peach Melba Escoffier originally prepared for Dame Nellie was *not* a Sundae, lacking both sauce (save for any drips from the liquid in which the peaches had been poached) and a small red fruit on top. But it's an absolute that when Escoffier added the raspberry purēe and shredded almonds, it was truly a Sundae that was being served.

THE RECIPES

NELLIE MELBA SUNDAE

*V*oilā —Good vanilla ice cream, poached peaches and raspberry purēe are all one needs for a good Peach Melba. The swan is entirely optional.

POACHED PEACHES

ESCOFFIER'S IDEA WAS TO PLACE MATURE, PERFECTLY RIPENED PEACHES IN BOILING WATER FOR TWO SECONDS, REMOVE WITH A SLOTTED SPOON, AND PLACE THEM IN ICE WATER FOR A FEW SECONDS. PEEL, HALVE AND PIT THEM; SPRINKLE WITH A LITTLE SUGAR AND REFRIGERATE.

RASPBERRY PURÉE

RUB FRESH OR FROZEN AND DEFROSTED RASPBERRIES WITH THE BACK OF A LARGE SPOON THROUGH A FINE SIEVE SET OVER A MIXING BOWL. STIR IN SUPERFINE SUGAR AND KIRSCH (CHERRY BRANDY) TO TASTE. COVER TIGHTLY WITH PLASTIC WRAP AND REFRIGERATE UNTIL READY TO SERVE.

PEACH MELBA SUNDAE

DIP 3 LARGE SCOOPS OF VANILLA ICE CREAM INTO A TALL SUNDAE GOBLET, AND COVER WITH RASPBERRY SAUCE. ADD FRESH SLICED PEACHES, GARNISH WITH WHIPPED CREAM, AND PLACE A MARASCHINO CHERRY AT THE TOP.

-JAXSON'S, DANIA BEACH, FLORIDA

POUND CAKE MELBA

4 slices pound cake
Vanilla ice cream
4 poached peach halves

²/₃ cup grenadine syrup
¹/₂ cup toasted almonds, chopped

PLACE A SLICE OF POUND CAKE IN THE BOTTOM OF EACH OF FOUR DESSERT BOWLS. TOP EACH WITH A SCOOP OF VANILLA ICE CREAM AND THEN A PEACH HALF, CUT SIDE DOWN, ON THE ICE CREAM. LADLE GRENADINE SYRUP OVER THE TOP AND SPRINKLE WITH CHOPPED, TOASTED ALMONDS. SERVES 4.

– ANTOINE'S, NEW ORLEANS, LOUISIANA

FIT FOR A QUEEN—
CHERRIES JUBILEE

Many dishes were created in Queen Victoria's honor during her sixty-four-year reign, and Escoffier was asked to create a new dish in honor of Her Royal Majesty's Diamond Jubilee. He chose cherries as a key ingredient. Cherries Jubilee flamed into culinary history in 1897, and has flickered in and out of style since. Almond flavoring is the secret to this version of Cherries Jubilee.

1 cup sugar
2 cups water
1¹/₂ pounds pitted black cherries
1 tablespoon cornstarch

¹/₂ cup warm kirsch (cherry
  brandy)
¹/₂ teaspoon almond extract
Vanilla ice cream

COMBINE SUGAR AND WATER IN A SAUCEPAN AND BRING TO A BOIL. ADD CHERRIES AND POACH UNTIL TENDER. DRAIN CHERRIES AND RESERVE ONE CUP OF THE LIQUID. ADD CORNSTARCH TO THE LIQUID AND STIR OVER MEDIUM HEAT UNTIL IT THICKENS. ADD THE CHERRIES AND ALMOND EXTRACT, AND STIR. WHEN READY TO SERVE, CAREFULLY POUR THE BRANDY INTO THE PAN. LET IT HEAT FOR 30 SECONDS, THEN IGNITE A LARGE KITCHEN MATCH AND TOUCH IT TO THE PAN'S INGREDIENTS TO FLAME THE SAUCE. SPOON THE FLAMING CHERRIES OVER THE ICE CREAM, ALONG WITH SOME OF THE PAN LIQUID.

SAFETY ADVICE: BE CAREFUL! PLEASE FLAME THIS DESSERT ONLY IF YOU HAVE TAKEN THE PROPER PRECAUTIONS. YOU SHOULD HAVE AN EXTINGUISHER, FOR

ONE THING, AS WELL AS AN EXHAUST HOOD. MAKE SURE THERE'S NOTHING FLAM-
MABLE NEARBY AND STAND BACK. THE INITIAL FLAME CAN BE QUITE A BURST!

WAFFLE WORKS

*B*elgian waffles and ice cream go way back in Europe although it's more common in northern Europe to find the waffle served with whipped cream and berries or, in France, a sugary chestnut spread. Be that as it may, it took a dollop of American creativity to come up with waffle Sundaes.

This Sundae incorporates baked apple slices, waffles, which can be made before or while the apples bake, and kept warm, vanilla ice cream, hot caramel sauce, whipped cream and cherries for the top.

BAKED APPLE SLICES

6 Golden Delicious apples, peeled, $^{1}/_{2}$ cup sugar
cored and sliced $^{1}/_{4}$ cup butter
 $^{1}/_{2}$ cup apple juice

COMBINE APPLE JUICE, SUGAR AND BUTTER IN A LARGE SAUCEPAN AND HEAT UNTIL BUTTER IS MELTED. ADD APPLES AND COOK OVER MEDIUM HEAT UNTIL THE FRUIT IS TENDER, APPROXIMATELY 10-15 MINUTES. REMOVE FROM HEAT AND, USING A COLANDER WITH A BOWL UNDERNEATH TO CATCH THE JUICES, STRAIN APPLES. PLACE APPLES IN A BOWL AND SET ASIDE.

RETURN JUICES TO THE SAUCEPAN AND BOIL OVER MEDIUM HEAT UNTIL REDUCED AND SLIGHTLY THICKENED, ABOUT 2-5 MINUTES. ADD REDUCED JUICES TO THE APPLE SLICES AND STIR TO COAT. MAKES ENOUGH FOR 4 SUNDAES.

NOTE: IF NOT USING RIGHT AWAY, APPLES CAN BE REFRIGERATED IN AN AIR-TIGHT CONTAINER FOR UP TO 5 DAYS. REHEAT IN A SAUCEPAN OVER A LOW FLAME.

SUNDAE ASSEMBLY

PLACE TWO VANILLA ICE CREAM SCOOPS ATOP A WARM WAFFLE, THEN SMOTHER WITH WARM SLICED BAKED APPLES AND HOT CARAMEL SAUCE. TOP WITH WHIPPED CREAM AND A CHERRY.

- TWOHEY'S, ALHAMBRA, CALIFORNIA

Chapter 23

SOUTHERN SUNDAE HOSPITALITY

"In the South, we have a way of expanding our relatedness to other people through food."

– ELLEN ROLFES, *THE SOUTHERN CULTURE COOKBOOK*

From Little Rock, I followed Highway 67 North for about forty-five miles. I took Exit 42 onto Main Street, turned left at the White County Library, and on the next block a modest sign with red letters announced my arrival at the Yarnell Ice Cream Company, smack-dab in the middle of Searcy, Arkansas.

It was near the end of a particularly hot summer in 1932 when an ambitious young man named Ray Yarnell purchased a small, ten-year-old ice cream plant at this very spot. Those were the days before home freezers, when practically every town in Arkansas had its own ice cream plant. Yarnell's first trucks were cooled with ice and salt. Just like its ice cream freezers. Each morning, drivers had to chip ice by hand, then climb to the top of their trucks and dump it along with salt along the sides to keep the trucks cold.

"If you look closely at the truck in this picture, you'll notice the railing around the top," says Christina Yarnell, pointing to one of the photographs that line the walls of the company offices. "It kept the men from falling off while they loaded that ice and salt. On a long truck route, the men had to stop at ice houses in each town to add more ice and drain off the water."

Christina is the keeper of Yarnell's history. She is the fourth generation of the ice cream-making family, and its striking director of public relations. As a young girl, she listened to her grandfather, Albert, tell how he had made ice cream deliveries on his bicycle. Yarnell is run today by Christina's father, Rogers. "Family stories," Christina says, "are the bonds that keep families alive."

Because of family stories, Christina Yarnell can describe vividly the days well before her time. "In those times, remember, people couldn't keep ice cream at home,' she explains. "There was a special day of the year for ice cream—the Fourth of July. Our rural communities had no electricity, and country stores could not keep ice cream on hand. So the big Independence Day picnic was one of the few occasions in the year when folks could buy all the ice cream they could eat.

"Concession stands dotted the picnic grounds across the street from our plant, with ice cream packed in five-gallon tubs. Great-grandfather made just a few basic flavors, so local folks took to dressing up their dishes of ice cream with honey, molasses and homemade preserves, Sundae-style."

The little ice cream company began to grow at the end of the 1930s when Yarnell purchased its first electrically refrigerated truck. It held 650 gallons, and Ray's wife, Hallie, worried about whether their company would ever be able to sell so much ice cream.

Over the years, most of the community ice cream companies of Arkansas disappeared. Yarnell now not only dominates the ice cream market in its home state, but has grown to become a competitor from Texas to Mississippi. It employs two hundred and twenty-five people.

MIAMI BEACH KITSCH

*M*iami Beach is a delicious world unto itself and yet on its deco-chic shores can be found some of the best traditional Sundaes around anywhere—at Wolfie's, the iconic blue and pink Jewish deli. In big, booming business since 1947, Wolfie's, open 24 hours a day, offers huge, conversation-stopping Ice Cream Sundaes and banana splits. Bowls of sour dill pickles on the table preview any order, so neither a pregnant woman nor anyone else ever has to explain any urge. Wolfie's is big by day with many folks, and in the wee hours of the morning it's a fave of insomniacs and club kids.

Milk and cream for Yarnell's ice creams are delivered fresh from the dairy farmers' cooperative in northwest Arkansas three times a day, and tested for quality immediately upon arrival. The liquids are pumped into a holding tank, pasteurized, homogenized, then aged overnight. Following the addition of sugar with a high-speed blender, the mix is drawn into a flavor vat where fruit purées or colors are added. Next, the mix enters a "barrel" freezer where it is frozen as rotating dashers incorporate air. The result can now properly be called ice cream.

Fruits, nuts, candy, cookies, or other ingredients are added to the semi-frozen slurry, which has a consistency similar to soft-serve ice cream. Cartons travel down a conveyor system and slide onto a carousel where they are filled, capped, boxed, and shrink-wrapped by machine, before being whisked into the hardening room for blast freezing—the colder the temperature, the faster the hardening, the smoother the product. Finished products are stacked by flavor, sorted by orders, and loaded into Yarnell's fleet of refrigerated trucks, ready for delivery.

After I saw more ice cream than most people see in a lifetime, Christina suggested a place where I could put Yarnell's ice cream to the Sundae test. We drove a few blocks to a coffee house/restaurant called the Midnight Oil, next door to U-Haul. The bicycle parked outside belonged to Midnight Oil owner, Matthew West.

The interior presented a comfy setting with a dozen tables and forty or so chairs set on a hardwood floor, plus a large couch and overstuffed easy chairs around a fireplace. I'm told that Midnight Oil (yes, it's open that late) is popular with students from nearby Harding College; it also draws morning coffee and lunch-break regulars in the *Leave-it-to-Beaver* town of Searcy.

Matthew chatted with us. "We're in a dry county," he explained, "so folks in these parts stop by for a Sundae the way people in other places visit a bar." He says he selected the Homemade Vanilla for his establishment after trying all four Yarnell vanillas. "It's right in between the Angel Food Vanilla and not quite to French Vanilla," says West. "The creaminess holds up in Sundaes and shakes."

So what about that Sundae? The Midnight Oil's "Chocolate Sundae" arrived as plain as could be. A classic tulip held two scoops of the fresh, white ice cream, covered with Hershey's dark brown chocolate syrup, decorated with a mound of whipped cream (no cherry).

As I dug in with my tall spoon, before I even tasted the Sundae, I knew I'd like it. Visiting a town like Searcy, seeing ice cream made

UDDER TO UTTER EXPERIENCE

*B*raum's is the only major ice cream maker and retailer in the United States that milks its own cows.

Back in the Depression, Henry Braum was a Kansas dairy farmer with a small milk and butter processing plant. By 1940, he'd added ice cream-making to use up his milk surplus. After college, Henry's son, Bill, joined his dad in business and began to open retail ice cream stores.

In 1968, Bill Braum sold his 61 Peter Pan stores and moved lock, stock and barrel to Tuttle, Oklahoma. Today, the Braum dairy cows number 10,000 and graze on 40,000 acres. And Braum's Ice Cream operates 280 retail stores in Oklahoma, Texas, Kansas, Missouri and Arkansas.

Braum cows produce the milk that's made into Braum's ice cream, delivered in a Braum truck to a Braum's store, where you can enjoy a Braum's Strawberry Shortcake Sundae. Holy cow!

BRAUM'S COWS GRAZE OUTSIDE ITS ICE CREAM PLANT.

and finally sitting down to a Sundae was an emotional shortcut back to childhood comfort.

If there's magic in ice cream—and I sincerely believe there is—then Sundaes are the most magical of all.

CAJUN COURAGE

*F*olks from all over America have made the pilgrimage to Robin's in Henderson, Louisiana, thirty miles from Baton Rouge. They come for chef Lionel Robin's unpretentious Cajun specialties, perfected over three decades of restaurant cooking.

Robin's "Hot Chocolate Sundae" is not for faint hearts; its basis is Tabasco ice cream. The chef makes the ice cream with a standard vanilla recipe, to which he adds one ounce of pepper sauce for every quart of heavy cream. If you want to make this at home, he says, it's important to shake the bottle of Tabasco vigorously before releasing the sauce.

"After the first two or three bites" [of the ice cream], Robin says, "you begin to get the flavor of the Tabasco, which doesn't get any more hot."

To make the Sundae, he pours chocolate syrup over the Tabasco ice cream. "Chocolate and Tabasco go well together," he says encouragingly.

THE RECIPES

PRALINE SUNDAE

*P*ralines trace their origin to an 18th-century French chef who coated almonds in sugar for consumption as a digestive aid. By the mid-1800s, the recipe had made its way to New Orleans, where the sweet "medicine" was made with Louisiana pecans and sugar milled from local cane.

Pralines (please say "prah-leens") are now identified with New Orleans. Under the Praline syrup in this Sundae goes vanilla—or French vanilla, if you will—ice cream. Nothing more is needed.

PRALINE SAUCE

1 pound granulated sugar
1 cup dark corn syrup
¹/₂ cup water
¹/₂ cup twice-brewed black coffee

2 tablespoons butter
3 cups roasted pecan halves or
pieces

PLACE THE SUGAR IN A LARGE, HEAVY POT AND SET IT OVER MEDIUM HEAT. STIRRING OFTEN, SLOWLY LET THE SUGAR MELT AND CARAMELIZE UNTIL DARK BROWN, BEING CAREFUL NOT TO LET IT BURN. STIR IN THE DARK CORN SYRUP. ADD THE WATER ALONG WITH THE COFFEE AND BUTTER. BRING THE POT TO A BOIL, LOWER TO A SIMMER AND COOK, STIRRING OCCASIONALLY, FOR ABOUT 30 MINUTES. REMOVE THE POT FROM THE HEAT AND ALLOW IT TO COOL TO ROOM TEMPERATURE. IF THE SAUCE IS TOO THICK, ADD A LITTLE WATER. MAKES ABOUT 4 CUPS.

IF IT LOOKS AS IF YOU HAVE MORE SYRUP THAN YOU NEED, SET THE EXTRA ASIDE, WHICH WILL KEEP FOR A FEW WEEKS IN A TIGHTLY CLOSED CONTAINER. (IF YOU REFRIGERATE THE EXTRA, LET IT WARM TO ROOM TEMPERATURE BEFORE ITS NEXT USE.) ADD THE ROASTED PECANS TO THE SYRUP YOU'RE USING SHORTLY BEFORE SERVING SO THEY WILL MAINTAIN THEIR CRISPNESS.

– GUMBO SHOP, NEW ORLEANS, LOUISIANA

FROZEN MUG
SUNDAE

DIP 2 LARGE SCOOPS OF VANILLA ICE CREAM INTO A FROSTED BEER MUG, AND COVER WITH CHOICE OF TOPPINGS (HOT FUDGE SAUCE, CARAMEL SAUCE, CHOCOLATE SAUCE, CRUSHED STRAWBERRIES, BLUEBERRY SYRUP, OR SORGHUM MOLASSES). GARNISH WITH WHIPPED CREAM, SPRINKLE WITH ROASTED ALMONDS AND PLACE A MARASCHINO CHERRY AT THE TOP.

– CRACKER BARREL, LEBANON, TENNESSEE

Chapter 24

MEET ME IN ST. LOUIS

*"A Hot Fudge Sundae and a trashy novel
is my idea of heaven."*

– BARBARA WALTERS

*I*n Missouri, the Sundae has been pronounced "Sunduh" since way back when. So, how do you explain it? "Sunday is the day you go to church," says Andrew Karandzieff, "and a Sunduh is what you eat *after* you go to church."

He ought to know. Andrew, along with brothers Michael and Thomas, perpetuate the family legacy at a revered St. Louis relic called Crown Candy Kitchen. This candy and ice cream parlor has stood on the corner of St. Louis Avenue and 14th Street, pouring forth a stream of old-fangled Sundaes, for nearly nine decades.

If a business survives into ripe old age, it's called a tradition. Crown Candy has gone beyond that point to become a heartland institution. It continues to thrive in a section of north St. Louis that has seen better days. Crown Candy Kitchen is a wonderful anachronism. "Change is not a good thing," insists Andy Karandzieff.

Just after the turn of the last century, St. Louis was the third largest city in the United States, after New York and Philadelphia, and it had been the gateway to the West for decades. As the great wave of immigrants altered the character of America, a young Greek named Harry Karandzieff brought confectionery skills with him to St. Louis. At first he worked at a local shoe factory for $3 a day, but after two years he found a modest space where he could practice his candy-maker profession. He was a small man with big dreams, and his establishment became known for both its hand-rolled sweets and Ice Cream Sundaes.

If memory is not playing tricks on the Karandzieff clan, the store has been open every day since 1913, seven days a week, save for a few weeks following a fire on the day after Christmas, 1983.

If you were ever thinking about building a time machine to slide backward in American soda parlor history, don't bother. This place transforms you to another era—and sweeter times—the moment you step inside. Open the 14th Street door or the adjacent St. Louis Avenue door. You'll know you've stumbled onto genuine Americana as soon as you see all the Coca-Cola memorabilia hung on the walls for decoration. A few rays of late-morning sun accentuate the aged, off-white booths. They are exactly as they've always been, except for the backs. When the ladies who lunch on Sundaes in St. Louis complained that they were neither able to see nor be seen due to the booths' high backs, they were dragged out, sawed down and repainted over one weekend (the booths, not the ladies).

It's business as usual here. The Karandzieffs, grandsons three, work hand in hand, energized by the dedication of those who came before them. Tom is the tireless short-order cook who feeds a small army every day; Andy enthusiastically produces daily batches of ice cream, and takes special pride in his snow-white vanilla; Mike dances behind the counter, skillfully scooping Andy's freshly-made ice cream into cones, malts, and Sundaes.

George Karandzieff, son of the late founder, is fiercely proud of his three boys. "It warms my heart to have the whole family working

THE CROWN CANDY KITCHEN IN ST. LOUIS.

Since CROWN Candy KITCHEN 1913

here," he says. "I wish Harry was here to see it." Papa George reminisces while making Heavenly Hash, a candy brick of marshmallows, pecans, and milk chocolate. While he has turned over operation of the business to his sons, he continues to help in the production of candies and candy-style toppings for the Ice Cream Sundaes.

"It is strange how quickly ninety years can pass," says the elder Karandzieff. He remembers selling popcorn from a cart out in front of his father's store. "Our family has probably forgotten more about Sundae-making than most others will ever know," he adds, while tempering the chocolate with his large, experienced hands.

"This neighborhood was settled by waves of immigrants, first German, then Irish and later Italian, Polish and Jewish," he explains. "But the more the neighborhood changed over the years, the more Crown Candy stayed the same."

Crown Candy's present-day neighbors like Ice Cream Sundaes just as much as their predecessors did. And some of those who have moved away from Crown Candy have not forgotten it: They stop by, now and then, when tasks take them from the suburbs to the city; or, having moved farther away, they've passed on word about the Sundaes to those whose travels take them to St. Louis.

With all due respect to Tom, whose good sandwiches fill the function of slipping conscientious eaters dabs of carbohydrates, protein and vitamins (he never forgets the pickle chips) before they hit dessert, the Crown is about Ice Cream Sundaes. Its inspired list offers desserts in three defiantly ancient categories, long since vanished from most American soda fountains. A Sundae is ice cream and syrup, that's it; a Newport includes whipped cream and nuts; a Deluxe adds more flavors of ice cream and/or syrups.

The single greatest thing to eat at Crown Candy Kitchen is the Crown Sundae Deluxe. Devouring this grail of Sundaes is a near holy experience. Each Crown Sundae arrives with its house-made ingredients oozing over the edge; hot fudge competes with caramel sauce for your attention, if you're not gripped first by the butter-roasted pecans. This Sundae commands unyielding loyalty from customers. It's not unique. It's not hard to make. It's not particularly beautiful, but it has a little of all these things, and perhaps that's why it satisfies a lot of different people. Order a Crown Sundae and you won't believe for a moment that the Karandzieff family has forgotten one single thing about making Sundaes.

Sometimes it's a fair world: The best survives because it is the best. True Sundae achievement requires discipline and patience developed over time. "If it was easy," says George Karandzieff, sounding like Yogi Berra, "it wouldn't be this hard."

THE RECIPES

CANDY KITCHEN GREATS

CROWN DELUXE

DIP 2 LARGE SCOOPS OF VANILLA ICE CREAM INTO A TALL SUNDAE GOBLET. COVER WITH 2 OUNCES OF HOT FUDGE SAUCE AND 2 OUNCES OF CARAMEL SAUCE. SPRINKLE BUTTER-ROASTED PECANS OVER THE TOP.

FIRE CHIEF SPECIAL

DIP 2 LARGE SCOOPS OF VANILLA ICE CREAM SIDE BY SIDE INTO A WIDE SUNDAE BOWL. COVER ONE SCOOP WITH CHOCOLATE SYRUP, THE OTHER WITH CRUSHED STRAWBERRIES. PLACE ROUND SLICES OF BANANAS AROUND THE ICE CREAM. GARNISH WITH WHIPPED CREAM, SPRINKLE WITH CHOPPED PECANS AND CHOPPED CASHEWS, AND PLACE A MARASCHINO CHERRY AT THE TOP.

UNCLE SAM SUNDAE

DIP 2 LARGE SCOOPS OF VANILLA ICE CREAM SIDE BY SIDE INTO A WIDE SUNDAE BOWL. COVER ONE SCOOP WITH CRUSHED STRAWBERRIES, THE OTHER WITH CRUSHED PINEAPPLE. PLACE ROUND SLICES OF BANANAS AROUND THE ICE CREAM. GARNISH WITH WHIPPED CREAM, SPRINKLE WITH RED, WHITE, AND BLUE JIMMIES AND PLACE A MARASCHINO CHERRY AT THE TOP.

– CROWN CANDY KITCHEN, ST. LOUIS, MISSOURI

IOWA BLASTS
FROM THE PAST

*D*espite its cutting-edge name, the Space Sundae goes down very smoothly. Best of all, you can eat in a drugstore established when Abe Lincoln was president.

As for the High School Sundae, it has a special place in my heart because it's made with cherries, although it's more gussied up than that very first Sundae I've told you about. Wilton's, where it is served, was founded in 1910.

SPACE SUNDAE

Dip 2 large scoops of vanilla ice cream into a Sundae tulip. Ladle 2 ounces of chocolate syrup and 2 ounces of marshmallow syrup over the ice cream. Make it pretty with whipped cream and a sprinkling of chopped almonds before putting the cherry on top.

– Penn Drug, Sidney, Iowa

HIGH SCHOOL SUNDAE

Place 2 large scoops of vanilla ice cream into a Sundae tulip. Ladle on 2 ounces of cherries in syrup and 2 ounces of marshmallow syrup. Fancy up with whipped cream and a shower of Spanish peanuts.

– Wilton's Candy Kitchen, Wilton, Iowa

Chapter 25

THE ELECTRIC SUNDAE

"In real life, unlike in Shakespeare, the sweetness
of the rose depends upon the name it bears."
– HUBERT H. HUMPHREY

From just the right spot in Hamburg, Iowa, locals say, you can see all the way into Nebraska to the west and across Missouri to the south. Twelve hundred people populate this town on the Nishnabotna River, where the biggest employer is Vogel Popcorn. But Marge Bennett has worked at Stoner Drug for four decades. At Stoner, a bag of locally grown, locally popped corn goes for a quarter.

But I hadn't telephoned Marge to discuss local popcorn prices. I'd called because I'd heard that Stoner has a Fried Egg Sundae on its menu, and I wanted to find out how to make one. Marge told me that the Fried Egg Sundae was not a cute breakfast item. It was a Sundae that, as she described it, sounded pretty good: Its center is a scoop of cream-colored vanilla ice cream covered with a marshmallow cream, which could be construed to resemble the yolk of an easy-over egg, and it is ringed with chocolate sauce that might remind you of the browned edges of the white.

But why would someone want to think about a fried egg when he ate a Sundae? Marge couldn't answer that. She recalled that the Sundae had been thought up by Jean Gude, a girl who had been a waitress with her when they were both in high school. They'd had the customers who filled the twelve stools at the marble-topped fountain to look after, as well as the ones who occupied the four booths, and while that kept them busy most of the time, there were still some idle moments when they could let their imaginations fly. It was during such a moment that Jean had been visited by her vision of a Sundae that looked like a fried egg.

Marge couldn't recollect more and she didn't know where Jean Gude might be, these forty years later. She did add, "Occasionally, someone is curious enough to order one, but the Fried Egg Sundae never really caught on."

Marge's boss, who had also been Jean's boss, Marvin Volertsen, admitted, "I can't recall ever seeing one of those things being made." Marvin, a pharmacist, bought the drugstore from his father-in-law, Ralph Stoner, in 1953. Marvin wanted me to tell you that in 1957 he'd moved the fountain and booths from the original 1896 pharmacy to Stoner's current location, and now I have.

I collect curious Sundae names, as you've probably ascertained, and while I'm sometimes lucky enough to find out what goes into these curios, only rarely do I get as close to what was going on in the mind of the actual name-giver as I did with the help of Marge. Thank you, Ms. Bennett. And Jean Gude, wherever you are, I salute you.

Many Sundaes have "humorous titles," which is how William S. Adkins described the odd names of some ice cream concoctions in a 1933 issue of *Druggists Circular*. Adkins suggested a dish called the "Electric Sundae." Among the virtues he saw for such a Sundae is that it could be "advertised as having plenty of juice and currants." He went on to explain how to make it and who would appreciate it: "Fruit syrup is poured over ice cream and sprinkled with currants. A novelty of this nature goes well at a college grill, young blades deriving infinite entertainment through explaining the proposition to each newcomer."

Interestingly, Adkins came to the game of advising druggists and soda clerks rather late. In the early part of the 20th century, *The*

A FRIED EGG SUNDAE AT STONER'S DRUG IN HAMBURG, IOWA.

Dispenser's Formulary was already passing on the accumulated wisdom of "counter culture" and encouraging soda jerks to let great events inspire their Sundae names. One dazzling, icy event was a natural.

After several unsuccessful attempts to reach the North Pole, the American explorer Robert E. Peary sailed north on the 184-ton Roosevelt for another try. Peary drove a dogsled four hundred miles from his ship and stood at the North Pole on April 6, 1909. The cold was so intense, as he told it, that a flask of brandy carried under his parka froze solid. Six years later, *The Dispenser's Formulary* described not one, but two Sundaes, commemorating Peary's Arctic conquest.

"ROOSEVELT" SPECIAL

At one end of a banana boat place a large scoop of strawberry ice cream, and at the other, a large scoop of vanilla ice cream (strawberry represents the ship, vanilla represents an iceberg). Cover the vanilla with crushed pineapple, and the strawberry with red raspberries and chopped mixed nuts. Place two Nabisco wafers on the edge, one on either side of the strawberry ice cream, and pointing toward the vanilla. Then, put two Nabiscos in a vertical position on top of the strawberry for sails.

NORTH POLE SUNDAE

Split one large banana lengthwise, and arrange on a long plate to represent the runners of a sleigh. On these and to represent a "pack" add one large scoop of vanilla ice cream, and to simulate the snow effect, cover the "pack" with marshmallow syrup. On one end of the plate put a small candy polar bear; at the other end, put 6 small jelly gum drops. On top of the ice cream place a small American flag.

Sundae naming was something of an American mania in the decades before World War II. Fixing names to particular Sundae recipes both established their identities and created the expectation of uniformity. Once drugstore owners and their kind discovered that they might increase sales by offering novel Sundaes, the fun of naming became too important to be left exclusively to creative soda jerks.

OF MORE THAN ACADEMIC INTEREST

Even the places where the most whimsically named Sundaes are presented usually have staid names themselves, the name of the founder being the most usual. The second most popular choice incorporates the word, Sundae, as in Sundae City, Always Sundae, Everyday is Sundae, Once Upon a Sundae and Lazy Sundae. I find this a good sign, as it means the proprietors have Sundaes on their minds.

"The name says it all," said Paul Endres, as he finished posing for a photo with the entire staff of his first store in Dennisport, Massachusetts, in celebration of its twenty-fifth anniversary. Endres was a local schoolteacher when he decided to open an ice cream shop in his Cape Cod town, to make some extra money during the summer. He named it Sundae School. It was too appropriate to pass up.

He now owns three Cape Cod Sundae Schools, each sporting a vintage marble soda fountain. And he is an exacting schoolmaster, seeing to it that the berries on his Sundaes are fresh-picked from a local farm and that every Sundae has a fresh Bing cherry on top.

Fountain owners conducted Sundae popularity contests, new recipe contests and name-the-Sundae contests.

To my mind, the best Sundaes are quick works of simple art, logically and carefully composed, with the best ingredients. First comes the visual satisfaction, then the name. But the final test is the taste. The cleverest name in the world can't raise a Sundae with inferior ingredients to stardom, but assuming the best components, a memorable name makes a Sundae stick in your mind long after you've enjoyed it with your ice-cream spoon.

For your edification, I've charted some Sundaes names that tickle me. It's up to you to decide which Sundaes you want to seek out or recreate.

ADVERTISEMENT FOR OLD SMOOTHIE BRAND CHOCOLATE SYRUP.

SUNDAE COSTUME

*F*rom Lafayette, Louisiana, comes the story of Louis Albright, who decided to disguise himself as a Sundae before he robbed a bank. It was, he must have thought as he sprayed himself with commercial whip, an ingenious, low-cost (if high-fat), easily disposable cover-up. Plus, with his face masked in whipped cream, he could still say clearly, "Put all your money in the sack!" which were the very words he shot at the teller. Unfortunately for him, he hadn't considered the melt factor. As he stood awaiting the dough, the whip ran into his eyes and prevented him from noticing the teller push the silent alarm. This human Sundae was struggling with his meltdown when the police arrived.

SUNDAE CHART

Name	SOUTHERN COMFORT	COOKIE MAN	IDIOT'S DREAM
Ice Cream Flavor(s)	Vanilla	Cookies 'n' Cream	Pistachio
Syrups(s)	Caramel	Marshmallow Chocolate	Marshmallow, Bing Cherry
Add-Ons	Chopped Pecans, Pignola and Pistachio Nuts, Whipped Cream	Whipped Cream, Crushed Oreos	Whipped Cream, Sugar Wafers
Who	Nixon's Drugs	Mary Coyle's	Punch & Judy Ice Cream Parlor
Where	Mobile, AL	Phoenix, AZ	Los Angeles, CA

LUXURA	BUCKET OF WORMS	PIZZA	BITTERS GLOWING
Vanilla	Vanilla	Vanilla (spread two inches deep over 8-inch-round brownie)	Rum Raisin
Chocolate, Butterscotch	Chocolate	Chocolate or Caramel or Marshmallow	Angostura Bitters
Angel-Food Cake, Whipped Cream, Butter-roasted Pecans	Whipped Cream, Crushed Oreos, Gummy Worms	Nestlē Crunch, &/or Crushed Oreos, &/or Peanuts, &/or M & Ms	
Stevens Ice Cream	Wilderness Grill *Open*	Jennifer's Ice Cream *Open*	Trader Vic's *Open*
Los Angeles, CA	Ontario, CA	East Haven, CT	Honolulu, HI

Sundae Chart

Name	BROWN BOMBER	PMS	C'EST SI BON
Ice Cream Flavor(s)	Chocolate	Chocolate	Vanilla Strawberry
Syrups(s)	Chocolate	Hot Fudge	Marshmallow
Add-Ons	Whipped Cream	Chocolate Chips, Cookie Dough, Brownie Pieces, Whipped Cream	Banana, Strawberries, Mixed Nuts. Coconut Macaroon, Whipped Cream, Cashews
Who	Zephyr Café *Open*	Mango's *Open*	Lagomarcino Confectionery *Open*
Where	Chicago, IL	DeKalb, IL	Moline, IL

WHITE TRASH	POT HOLE	GOLD BRICK	ONE FREE HOUR IN THE CANDY STORE
Ice Cream Sandwich, quartered	Vanilla	Vanilla	Vanilla
Hershey's Syrup	Hot Fudge	Chocolate	Hot Fudge
Ersatz Whipped Cream	Chocolate Cake Crumbs	Toasted Almonds, French Fan Biscuit	Reese's Pieces, M & Ms, Whipped Cream
Redbones	Gifford's	Caucus Club	Eveready Diner
Somerville, MA	Skowhegan, ME	Detroit, MI	Hyde Park, NY

SUNDAE CHART, CONTINUED

Name	SAD EYED LADY	MEXICAN	REAGAN'S JELLYBEANER
Ice Cream Flavor(s)	Vanilla	Vanilla	Your Choice
Syrups(s)	Chocolate, Marshmallow	Chocolate	
Add-Ons	Whipped Cream	Spanish Peanuts	Whipped Cream, Red, White & Blue Jelly Beans
Who	Liberty Ice Cream Concern	Eddie's	Itgen's Ice Cream Parlor
Where	New York, NY	Sylvan Beach, NY	Valley Stream, NY

GUNSLINGER	TEDDY BEAR	APPLE PIE	FLOOD OF '36
Vanilla	Vanilla	Vanilla	Vanilla
Chocolate , Marshmallow	Hot Fudge, Marshmallow		"Mud" Fudge
Crushed Raspberries, Whipped Cream 🍒	Chopped Peanuts, Whipped Cream 🍒	Apple Pie Foundation, Whipped Cream 🍒	Crushed Oreos, Chocolate Jimmies, Whipped Cream 🍒
Hawthorne Sundae Saloon *Open*	Ednamae's *Open*	Galileo's Bar and Grill *Open*	Klavon's Ice Cream Parlor *Open*
Escondido, NC	Vermilion, OH	Oklahoma City, OK	Pittsburgh, PA

SUNDAE CHART, CONTINUED

Name	JOE SENT ME	BLACK DIAMOND SUNDAE	GRILLED POUND CAKE HOT FUDGE SUNDAE
Ice Cream Flavor(s)	Vanilla	Chocolate	Vanilla
Syrups(s)	Hot Fudge	Chocolate	Hot Fudge
Add-Ons	Crushed Strawberries, Whipped Cream, Chocolate Sprinkles	Whipped Cream	Pound Cake (grilled in butter) Foundation, Whipped Cream
Who	Sweet Dreams Café	People's Drugstore	Etta's Deli & Ice Cream Parlor
Where	Stroudsburg, PA	Washington, D.C.	Madison, WI

Lalapalooza

Vanilla

Marshmallow

Banana Slices,
Crushed
Strawberries,
Crushed
Pineapple ,
Roasted
Pecans

Gilles Custard
Stand

Milwaukee, WI

THE RECIPES

PIG DINNER SUNDAE

If you finish this one on the premises of its creator, you get a button that says, "I made a pig of myself at Sherman's."

LINE A WOODEN CONTAINER SHAPED LIKE A PIG'S TROUGH WITH WAXED PAPER. SPLIT ONE LARGE BANANA LENGTHWISE AND PLACE ON THE BOTTOM OF THE TROUGH. ADD ONE LARGE SCOOP EACH OF VANILLA, CHOCOLATE, STRAWBERRY AND BUTTER PECAN ICE CREAM ON TOP. LADLE 2 OUNCES EACH OF CHOCOLATE SAUCE, MARSHMALLOW SYRUP, CRUSHED STRAWBERRIES AND CRUSHED PINEAPPLE OVER THE SCOOPS. GARNISH WITH WHIPPED CREAM, SPRINKLE WITH CHOPPED MIXED NUTS AND PLACE 5 MARASCHINO CHERRIES ACROSS THE TOP.

– SHERMAN'S DAIRY BAR, SOUTH HAVEN, MICHIGAN

DYSFUNCTIONAL SUNDAE

ON A 13-INCH PLATE, PLACE A LARGE BROWNIE SQUARE AND POUR 2 OUNCES OF AMARETTO OVER THE TOP. HEAT IN THE MICROWAVE UNTIL WARM. DIP ONE LARGE SCOOP OF VANILLA ICE CREAM ONTO THE BROWNIE, LADLE HOT FUDGE OVER THE ICE CREAM AND SPRINKLE CHOPPED WALNUTS ON TOP. COVER WITH WHIPPED CREAM AND A SWIRL OF RASPBERRY PUREE.

– AFTERWARDS CAFÉ, WASHINGTON, D.C.

TOP HAT SUNDAE

PLACE THE BOTTOM HALF OF A LIGHT PASTRY SHELL ON A MEDIUM-SIZED PLATE. FILL WITH 2 LARGE SCOOPS OF VANILLA ICE CREAM AND COVER WITH THE TOP HALF OF PUFF PASTRY. DRIZZLE HOT FUDGE SAUCE ON TOP OF THE PASTRY, GARNISH WITH WHIPPED CREAM, AND PLACE A MARASCHINO CHERRY AT THE TOP.

– SUGAR BOWL, SCOTTSDALE, ARIZONA

Chapter 26

HOW SUNDAES WON THE WEST

"If Congress tried to forbid the eating of Ice Cream Sundaes or cotton candy, many people would be outraged; others would simply laugh."

– *MARIJUANA TIMES*

Who first put the Sundae *inside* ice cream? William Dreyer and Joseph Edy, it's time for your bow. This bold move was made in Jack London's hometown of Oakland, California. Oakland is also where Gertrude Stein was raised. While she was living in Paris with Alice B. Toklas of marijuana-brownie fame, Gertrude quipped of Oakland, "There's no *there*, there." Witty but wrong.

Dreyer and Edy opened the Grand Ice Cream Company, both factory and parlor, in Oakland in 1928. German-born Dreyer brought with him his experience as an ice cream maker at an ice creamery in Visalia, deep in the heart of California's dairy country. Joseph Edy had learned candy making at the side of his mother in Montana.

The Great Depression was a rough road to travel. Dreyer and Edy faced it with the brilliant notion of adding nuts and marshmallows to a batch of chocolate ice cream. First, they experimented with walnuts, but these tainted the ice cream with a bitter aftertaste. So they switched to lightly roasted almonds, which stayed sweet and crisp in the ice cream. Since miniature marshmallows did not yet exist, Edy used his wife's sewing shears, regularly dipped into hot water, to cut standard marshmallows into bite-size bits.

"Dreyer and Edy named their creation Rocky Road, not only because it described the mouth-feel of the flavor they had created, but because they believed it was a comment on the times," says John Harrison, Dreyer's Grand Ice Cream's official taster. "It's the Willy Wonka job," he says. Harrison looks his part; he stands nearly six feet tall, car-

A DREYER'S DRIVER CRANKS UP A DELIVERY TRUCK IN A CIRCA 1930 PHOTO.

ries his 245 pounds in jaunty steps, and is often smiling.

Like Clark Kent, who ducked into a phone booth to transform himself into Superman, Harrison puts on his white laboratory coat and black bow tie early each morning to prepare for the day's tastings. He avoids eating spicy foods or wearing aftershave, whose odors could compromise the sensitivity of his taste buds. Harrison is determined to save mankind from inferior ice creams.

He tastes vanilla first to clear the palate, then fastidiously works his way through flavors of more textural complexity: chocolate chip cookie dough and mint chocolate chip. With a gold spoon clasped firmly in hand, he scoops a small amount off the top of a half-gallon carton to test for taste, then digs deeper to test for body and texture. "First, I put a sample on my tongue," explains Harrison. "Then I aerate it by smacking my lips and bringing in the ambient room temperature, warming it up some more and driving that top bouquet up to the olfactory nerve. After I roll it around for four or five seconds, I spit it into a 55-gallon trash barrel." Like a wine taster, Harrison doesn't swallow what he tests, so that satiety doesn't become a judgment factor. And he finishes tastings by late morning to avoid palate fatigue.

Harrison is also Dreyer's developer of new flavors. He knows what we like to eat before we like it. In 1983, he was eating a scoop of vanilla along with a plate of cookies in the company's ice cream parlor when he thought to himself, "Why not save a step and put a cookie in the ice cream?" He experimented with fifteen brands of cookies before he determined that Oreos matched best with the ice cream. The Dreyer's marketing team came up with the name, Cookies 'n' Cream, and now it's the fifth best-selling flavor in America.

Asked what flavors he has rejected, Harrison answers without hesitation: "I once tried jalapeno pepper ice cream, but the hot and cold collided in a way I do not care to remember." He also admits to testing

MASSACHUSETTS INSPIRATION/TEXAS CRUSH

In Austin, Houston or San Antonio, you can live it up at Amy's Ice Cream with one of Amy Miller's "Crush In" sort-of Sundaes. This is an ice cream deal in which the customer's choices of nuts, cookies, candy and fruit bits are stirred into their scoops of ice cream before their eyes. Texans usually choose Mexican Vanilla Bean as their ice-cream base.

"Most ice cream dishes are served too cold, and they freeze the taste buds," Miller says, explaining the appeal of the Crush In. Plus her countermen and counterwomen tend to be as talented with their Sundae spades as cowpokes are with lassos, and so they're fun to watch.

Amy got her Crush In inspiration in the 80s when she was a student working at Steve Herrell's ice cream shop in Sommerville, Mass. Steve had invented the concept, which he called the "Smoosh-In." Steve, the man behind premium brand, Steve's Ice Cream, now runs Herrell's Ice Cream in Cambridge, Mass., where educated tasters say some of the best Sundaes in New England are served.

Amy ran with the Steve's smoosh idea when she moved to Texas to make her fortune. "It's impossible not to be cheerful selling ice cream," says Amy. "I love the job."

WESTWARD HO

Just after the dawning of the 20th century, Christian Anthony Fosselman tasted ice cream for the first time at a bottler's convention in Toronto. He was so impressed that he returned to Waverly, Iowa, and started making the stuff with the blessing of ice chunks from the river, which was frozen most of the winter. Before summer came, he and his men hauled in enough ice to keep the ice cream cold in his sawdust insulated sheds. The second good thing Christian recognized when it came about was refrigeration.

Refrigeration allowed him to move his business to Pasadena, California, in 1924. And there Fosselman's resides, often advertised by Sundae signs. Chris and John Fosselman base their award-winning ice creams on their grandfather's recipes. There's no telling what a week in Toronto will do for a farm-belt boy and his heirs.

out the old wives' tale about expectant mothers' craving for pickles and ice cream. He winces at the memory. "We like our ice cream, we like our pickles, but not together."

Although an adventurer by trade, Harrison also is loyal to the classics. "I love to sit down, eat a good Banana Split, and let the blues go," he confides. "It's a comfort food like no other in the world."

"The matrix of a real Sundae is the best possible vanilla ice cream," continues Harrison. "It ought to have the appearance of cream—not stark white, not bright yellow. As for flavor, the balance of dairy note, sugar, and added ingredients is critical. And the body must be clean and free of coarseness or icy crystals, the texture chewy but not gummy." Vanilla is his favorite flavor.

Dreyer's still operates the parlor at its original College Avenue location, in the same building that serves as corporate headquarters. Vanilla and Rocky Road anchor the Sundaes it sells there.

In recent years, Wild Blueberry has become a flavor almost as identified with the West as Rocky Road long has been.

CALIFORNIA SUNDAE DREAMING

Dolores Martinez only dreamed of banana splits when she was growing up in a large, poor Oakland family. Then at age 22, she got a secure night job at the Post Office and her world became a delicious place. Her delight was an after-work, breakfast banana split served at an Oakland coffee shop, Miz Brown's. For the first six months of her job, she ate the split for breakfast three times each week. "It was $3.25, which was expensive for a Sundae then, but worth it," remembers Ms. Martinez, who is tall and slender. "I'd go behind the counter and pick the banana I wanted: a big one with no bruises. The Sundae had three scoops of ice cream, three different sauces, nuts, whipped cream, cherries; it was big and it was perfect."

Ms. Martinez married and brought her new husband to Miz. Brown's. Even he was impressed although he'd grown up in a suburban home where ice cream was always in the freezer. After their first son, Danny, came along, they kept ice cream and syrup stocks at home. But frozen yogurt replaced the ice cream after they vowed to promote healthy eating at home.

Still, there are special occasions. Miz Brown's is gone, but Dolores has discovered the old-time Oakland parlor, Fentons Creamery, which specializes in huge Sundaes, such as The Works, which require three or four enthusiastic eaters to polish it off. Two years ago, Danny celebrated his junior high school graduation there.

And Ms. Martinez sometimes treats her seven-year-old son, Alex, to small Sundaes. "Near Halloween, Baskin Robbins offered this freaky little Sundae, which Alex loved," she says.

"I still dream of banana splits; I just don't want to set a bad example in front of the kids. But Oakland has great ice cream parlors, and one of these days when I have some free time all to myself, I'm going to go to one and order a great big banana split."

ROCKY MOUNTAIN
GOOD TIMES

Liks (né Lickety Split in 1976) throws Denver's best Sundae parties. Many enjoy Liks Sundaes in its splendid shop, but owner Jay Thompson reports that catered ice cream bashes at private parties, charity dos or company picnics are one way to beat the long lines outside his institution.

For groups of thirty or more, Thompson's crew pre-dips any three ice creams (from a list of 250 flavors, believe it or not!) and ladles up any three toppings (from a not quite so long list of favorites), then packs it all up with whipped cream, cherries, and plenty of dry ice to keep everything cold and delivers it to as far away as Boulder. The tab is a modest $2.85 per person.

"Six hundred people attended our biggest Sundae party," boasts Thompson. "Our most unusual affair was a fabulously indulgent pool party in downtown Denver—the adults got very creative with the whipped cream and cherries."

Catered "Sundae Socials" are also popular in New England and Pennsylvania—especially in the summer, and not only for children. What an entertaining way to entertain!

While it's likely that blueberry syrup was first thought up by an innovator from Blue Hill, Maine (it's the blueberries that give the hill its summer color), or elsewhere on northeastern shores, it's unlikely that anybody does Wild Blueberry Sundaes better than Hot Licks in Fairbanks, Alaska.

I like to think of this Sundae as the Last Frontier Sundae, although other wild berry Sundaes—whose ice creams or syrups are made with wild berries—are also popular in Alaska and down through Canada to Washington and Montana.

Boston-born Geoffrey Wool moved up to Alaska, attracted by the wild for many of the same reasons as earlier pioneers. He was a school-teacher then, but missed the ice cream of his native territory. So Wool decided to do his prospecting in ice cream and opened Hot Licks in 1986. He opted to put the "gold" in "them thar" ice creams himself. From the beginning, he produced super-premium ice creams.

Looking for your fortune in ice cream in Alaska could seem outlandish to outlanders. Do people really want to eat ice cream when it's 50 degrees F. below zero?

They do, Wool confirms. "It's so cold outside that the ice cream seems warm by comparison."

Hot Licks ice creams are handmade, forty quarts at a time, and sold throughout the Arctic Circle state. In summer, blueberries are ripe from Alaska's coastal rain forests to its tundra. Eating them in every way under the midnight sun in a seasonal ritual.

VANCOUVER VARIATIONS

*O*ne of the best-looking, old-time-styled eateries anywhere is the Sunshine Diner in Canada's queenly Pacific City. Red booths stand out handsomely against the sparkling black-and-white-square patterned floors; chrome fittings are everywhere. Back in the '50s, some Sunshine servers wore roller skates to assure, speedy smooth delivery; today they wear roller blades. The dessert menu is a simple match to the decor. You can have your "Sundae with chocolate or strawberry," and that's that.

The menu is more complex at the Hawaiian Café in Vancouver, where stir-fry of many Asian origins rules. Dessert jets you back to the Western Hemisphere: pride of place goes to the "Dutch Holland Chocolate Sundae." And just who is so merrily mixing up culinary traditions? The café's owner, an émigré from Honolulu, reflecting the mélange of Oahu, likes it hot and cold.

THE RECIPES

BLACK AND TAN SUNDAE

DIP ONE LARGE SCOOP OF VANILLA ICE CREAM AND ONE LARGE SCOOP OF ROCKY ROAD ICE CREAM SIDE-BY-SIDE INTO A WIDE SUNDAE BOWL. COVER THE VANILLA WITH CHOCOLATE SAUCE, AND THE ROCKY ROAD WITH CARAMEL SAUCE. GARNISH WITH WHIPPED CREAM, SPRINKLE WITH CHOPPED MIXED NUTS AND PLACE A CHERRY AT THE TOP.

– DREYER'S ICE CREAM SHOPPE, OAKLAND, CALIFORNIA

ALASKA WILD BLUEBERRY SUNDAE

This Sundae is about the syrup, so that's what this recipe is for. You spoon the syrup over vanilla ice cream and you're done.

4 cups blueberries	1 tablespoon cornstarch
1 cup sugar	$^1/_2$ cup water

BLUEBERRY SYRUP

MASH HALF THE BLUEBERRIES AND LEAVE THE OTHER HALF WHOLE. IN A SAUCEPAN MIX ALL INGREDIENTS. COOK OVER MEDIUM HEAT, STIRRING OCCASIONALLY, UNTIL SUGAR IS DISSOLVED AND SAUCE THICKENS. CHILL BEFORE USE. MAKES ABOUT 3 CUPS. POUR OVER VANILLA ICE CREAM.

– HOT LICKS, FAIRBANKS, ALASKA

CHOCOLATE JALAPENO SUNDAE

This is the signature dessert at the Tucson restaurant of Janos Wilder, a 2000 James Beard Award winner. Tiny snips of jalapeno are added to a vanilla ice cream recipe to make this Sundae base. The principle is the same as adding, say, chocolate chips, but you might want to use pepper bits more sparingly. Wilder's Sundae reflects the Mexican tradition of combining spicy and sweet, hot and cold.

• •

PLACE ONE LAYER OF WHITE CHOCOLATE GANACHE (EQUAL PARTS OF MELTED WHITE CHOCOLATE AND CREAM) INTO A TALL, PRE-CHILLED SUNDAE GOBLET, THEN ADD 3 LARGE SCOOPS OF JALAPENO ICE CREAM. SPRINKLE WITH SUGARED PECANS AND COVER WITH HOT FUDGE SAUCE. GARNISH WITH WHIPPED CREAM AND PLACE A CHILI-SHAPED COOKIE AT THE TOP.

• •

- JANOS, TUCSON, ARIZONA

DUSTY ROAD SUNDAE

• •

DIP 2 LARGE SCOOPS OF COFFEE ICE CREAM INTO A TALL SUNDAE GOBLET, AND COVER ICE CREAM WITH HOT FUDGE SAUCE. SPRINKLE WITH ONE HEAPING TABLESPOON OF MALTED-MILK POWDER, GARNISH WITH WHIPPED CREAM AND PLACE A CHOCOLATE-COVERED COFFEE BEAN AT THE TOP.

• •

- THE FORT, DENVER, COLORADO

RIDE INTO THE SUNSET

𝔅ob Farrell, the founder of the Oregon-based Farrell's Ice Cream Parlour chain, grew up in Brooklyn. "In Brooklyn, there were little ice cream stores on every corner; a fountain, candies, little café tables and stools," Farrell told an interviewer for *Lifestyles Northwest.* "I missed ice cream when I moved to Portland. I could die for Hot Fudge Sundaes."

Farrell's biggest Sundae creation was the Portland Zoo, which fed ten to fifteen and was ceremoniously delivered to the table on a hospital stretcher doubling as a tray.

In 1975, Farrell sold his 150-store empire to the Marriott Corporation, which withdrew from the restaurant business seven years later and disbanded the chain. Individually owned "parlours" bearing his name live on in Portland, San Diego, Los Angeles and Washington, D.C.

Many of Bob Farrell's customers wanted to have their Sundaes and their cakes, too. These two recipes date from the mid '60s .

TWO ON A BLANKET

DIP ONE LARGE SCOOP EACH OF VANILLA AND CHOCOLATE ICE CREAM SIDE-BY-SIDE ON A SLICE OF POUND CAKE. LADLE HOT FUDGE SAUCE OVER THE VANILLA AND MARSHMALLOW SYRUP OVER THE CHOCOLATE. GARNISH WITH WHIPPED CREAM, SPRINKLE WITH CHOPPED MIXED NUTS AND PLACE A MARASCHINO CHERRY AT THE TOP OF EACH SCOOP.

APPLE PANDOWDY

DIP 2 LARGE SCOOPS OF VANILLA ICE CREAM INTO A TALL SUNDAE GOBLET. COVER WITH HOT SLICED BAKED APPLES AND CRUMBLES OF CRISPY-BAKED PIE DOUGH. GARNISH WITH WHIPPED CREAM, DUST WITH NUTMEG, AND PLACE A CHERRY AT THE TOP.

– FARRELL'S ICE CREAM PARLOURS

YOU CAN BET ON IT

"Where else do you have the freedom to get up at four in the afternoon or four in the morning? Where else do you have the freedom to have a Hot Fudge Sundae for breakfast?" – THEME OF LAS VEGAS VISITORS AUTHORITY

Chapter 27

NEVER ON SUNDAE

"Is this idiocy? Or something so brilliant that it just looks stupid?"

– GARY KASPAROV

hile some Sundaes may be as deliberately thought out as a chess move, a few seem to me preposterous. Duncan Hines once suggested that he ran less risk driving his way across America than eating his way across it.

I've no problem, personally, with composed, stacked-food creations billed as Sundaes, although they've no ice cream. LA's ultra-cool Cadillac Café makes both a Turkey Sundae and a Mile-High Meatloaf Sundae. The Chili Sundae at Tony Packo's in Toledo, Ohio, challenges everything I know about Sundaehood. Just imagine a tall Sundae goblet filled with hot chili and sour cream in place of vanilla ice cream and syrup, shaved cheese as the alternative to whipped cream, and a cherry tomato on top instead of the you-know-what. I devoured this odd dish under a sign that read "The Worst Table in the House" (a table at the center of bottleneck traffic). Toledo native Jamie Farr, who played Corporal Klinger in the TV series, M.A.S.H., often expressed cravings for Packo's Hungarian hot dogs—both in and

CAN A SUNDAE KILL YOU?

idel Castro suspected it could. The Cuban leader has joked that he holds an "Olympic record" as an assassination plot target. Reportedly, he once dodged the bullet of a poison-spiked Chocolate Sundae served to him at a Havana hotel.

DOES YUCK MAKE THE MAN?

❦

*W*hen George Bush (senior) pledged a secret society at Andover Academy in Massachusetts, the hazing required ingestion of a Sundae no one but a scut would eat: a combo of ice cream, oysters and raw liver, garnished liberally with pepper. Did he know that a cast iron constitution would be needed for a far-future job?

out of his role. But even Farr concedes, "I have no idea why anyone would want a Chili Sundae."

Still, describing this dish as a Sundae is clearly meant as homage to the real thing. It's attention-getting, it's harmless—what the heck?

It's when I see or read about ice cream resting on or draped with some highly unlikely other foods that I stiffen. And when such a concoction is called a Sundae, my instant reaction here is that someone is trying to cash in on some culinary absurdity by stealing a Sundae's good name. But I suppose even dubious combinations are also salutes to America's greatest dessert.

Every Sundae recipe has a common origin: an entrepreneur who sees opportunity where others have missed it. Ice Cream Sundaes are not what they used to be, some moan; they consider franchise models poor facsimiles but don't know where to find good old-fashioned Sundaes, or haven't thought to make them at home.

Obviously, this book is meant to alter such an outlook. But in some instances, it's a good thing that Sundaes are not what they used to be,

ANYDAY . . . Have A Tony Packo's Chili Sundae

CHERRY TOMATOE

SHREDDED CHEDDAR CHEESE

SOUR CREAM

TONY PACKO HOT CHILI

The new combination that has 'em talking!

TONY PACKO'S CAFE

SOUR CREAM

TACO CHIPS

1902 Front St., Toledo
5827 Monroe St., Sylvania

because it isn't just recently that self-styled iconoclasts have introduced concoctions for which there isn't enough Alka-Seltzer in the world.

In 1944, Dick and Fred Farman formed the Farman Brothers Pickle Company in Tacoma, Washington, adopting the nickname "The Pickle People." Pickles have been their game ever since. Wouldn't you know it, the Pickle People came up with a Hot Pickle Sundae and the following instructions: Heat sweet mixed pickles and serve over scoop of vanilla ice cream.

Still, pickles and Sundaes (of a sort) are an old, rural upstate New York tradition. Fresh, hot maple syrup is poured onto clean snow, allowed to harden and served with donuts and pickles.

Maple syrup on snow was an early, easy Sundae throughout the northeastern sugar-maple region.

My vote for unlikeliest Sundae of all goes to the one once offered at the annual National Oyster Cook-Off in Baltimore by a competition

THIS IS A SUNDAE?

🍒

The Ponderosa chain in Atlantic Canada boasts that the soft-serve ice cream at its Sundae bar isn't real! No cow was the mother of its ice cream. No fat, no joy. But some claim that if you pile the toppings high enough—no difference.

Some urbane ice cream parlors throughout North America also stray from the basics—often to delicious effect. Yet there are occasions when, even though the ice cream is real enough, it's just not what you want in a Sundae. A trendy flavor such as green tea just doesn't take well to hot fudge.

Not that you can't be innovative and still get it right. The Brownie Ice Cream Sundae at Woolfy's in St. Mary's, Ontario, is made with sour cream ice cream.

Meanwhile, I'm still waiting for somebody over the age of ten to tell me why Nova Scotia's summer ice cream stands can't keep the flavor, Moon Mist, in stock. Little ones love it because it pretty much rolls the flavors of ice cream and cotton candy into one rainbow scoop. But it's also one of the few flavors that don't allow you to savor the creaminess of Canadian ice cream.

Open

DOG DAY SUNDAES

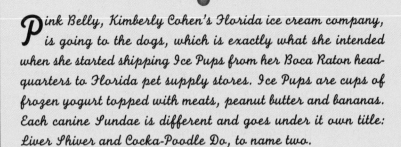

*P*ink Belly, Kimberly Cohen's Florida ice cream company, is going to the dogs, which is exactly what she intended when she started shipping Ice Pups from her Boca Raton headquarters to Florida pet supply stores. Ice Pups are cups of frozen yogurt topped with meats, peanut butter and bananas. Each canine Sundae is different and goes under it own title: Liver Shiver and Cocka-Poodle Do, to name two.

finalist who plumbed the depths of culinary creativity with a concoction of vanilla ice cream studded with breaded oysters, then drizzled with chocolate sauce.

Another curious Sundae is one proposed by Connie Berman and Suzanne Munshower in their book *Bagelmania*. The Hot Fudge Bagel Supreme perches a classic Hot Fudge Sundae atop a bagel that has been

soaked in crēme de cocoa. Connie told me that they included this because some people love dessert bagels, but she personally turns up her nose at "anything more elaborate than an onion or garlic bagel with chive and cream cheese spread."

Sometimes, even when a Sundae incorporates no unusual ingredient, more really should be less. Two Sisters a la Mode in Philadelphia offered a Sundae at the top of a milkshake. Kelly's Front Porch in Ocean City, Maryland, is willing to put a Sundae on the bottom of a milkshake.

ONLY AN HONEST *SUNDAE IS WORTH EATING ANY DAY OF THE WEEK.*

THE RECIPES

TASTY TOASTY SUNDAE

*I*ce cream and maple syrup is a Jeffersonian legacy; the addition of corn flakes is pure Americana. But this Sundae, even for breakfast, is a culinary faux pas.

DIP ONE LARGE SCOOP OF VANILLA ICE CREAM INTO A CEREAL BOWL. COVER THE ICE CREAM WITH MAPLE SYRUP AND THEN SPRINKLE CORN FLAKES OVER THE TOP.

– LIMA SANDWICH SHOP, LIMA, NEW YORK

HONEY-POACHED GARLIC SUNDAE

*J*oAnn Clevenger, gracious owner of the Upperline Restaurant in New Orleans, defends the garlic Sundae. She says, "We put garlic on a pedestal and hold a Garlic Festival [here] every June and July. The garlic Sundae will take your mind off the searing New Orleans heat."
I enjoyed the garlic in the initial and main courses of her wonderful restaurant, but one should never finish with garlic. If you hazard the following recipe, which serves six, remember to pass the Clorets!

½ pint honey	1 cinnamon stick
½ pint water	Curled peel of 1 lemon
10 peeled cloves garlic	1 quart vanilla ice cream

PLACE FIRST 5 INGREDIENTS TOGETHER IN A MEDIUM SAUCE PAN AND COOK GENTLY UNTIL THE WATER HAS EVAPORATED AND THE GARLIC HAS CARAMELIZED. REMOVE CINNAMON STICK AND LEMON PEEL, ALLOW MIXTURE TO COOL TO ROOM TEMPERATURE, THEN SPOON OVER ICE CREAM.

– UPPERLINE RESTAURANT, NEW ORLEANS, LOUISIANA

CHOP SUEY SUNDAE

J found this relic in an old collection of recipes submitted by soda jerks from around the country. I attempted to contact Peil's Soda Fountain in Honesdale, Pennsylvania, where this dish supposedly originated, but it is out of business. After trying out this misguided effort, I am not in the least bit surprised. What were they thinking in Honesdale?

¹/4 cup sugar	2 large scoops vanilla ice cream
¹/4 cup water	¹/4 cup flaked coconut
¹/4 cup raisins	¹/4 cup chow mein noodles
¹/4 cup chopped dates	

BOIL THE WATER AND SUGAR TOGETHER FOR 5 MINUTES, THEN ADD THE RAISINS AND DATES, STIR TO BLEND AND REMOVE FROM HEAT. POUR OVER THE ICE CREAM AND TOP WITH THE COCONUT AND NOODLES.

– PEIL'S SODA FOUNTAIN, HONESDALE, PENNSYLVANIA

HOT FUDGE BAGEL SUPREME

1 cinnamon-raisin bagel, sliced	3 tablespoons chopped walnuts
2 teaspoons dark crème de cacao	Dab of whipped cream
1 scoop vanilla ice cream	2 maraschino cherries
4 ounces hot fudge sauce	

TOAST BAGEL AND PRICK BOTH HALVES WITH A FORK. IN A SHALLOW DISH, SOAK BAGEL HALVES IN CRÈME DE CACAO FOR 15 MINUTES. PUT 1 BAGEL HALF, SLICED SIDE UP, IN A DESSERT DISH. TOP WITH ICE CREAM, THEN SECOND BAGEL HALF, SLICED SIDE DOWN. HEAT FUDGE TOPPING. POUR OVER BAGEL. TOP WITH NUTS, GARNISH WITH WHIPPED CREAM, AND PLACE MARASCHINO CHERRIES AT THE TOP.

– FROM *BAGELMANIA* BY CONNIE BERMAN AND SUZANNE MUNSHOWER

Chapter 28

SEX AND THE SUNDAE

*"Back when I was your age, I always made myself
a big banana split after sex.
I think you're gonna need one tonight."*

– MAGDA (LIN SHAYE) COUNSELING MARY (CAMERON DIAZ) IN
THERE'S SOMETHING ABOUT MARY BY PETER AND BOBBY FARRELLY

Sundaes are a joy in themselves, a consolation for disappointments (including romantic ones) and a seduction tool.

Food writer Teresa Lust once described the connection between food and desire as "the luxurious feel on the tongue of melting ice cream—there is no denying that some foods have the power to arouse the senses.

In *Much Depends On Dinner*, Margaret Visser points out that ice cream long has been seen as "female" in northern cultures. The breast-shaped scoop of ice cream in a cone or Sundae dish rests on a ragged edge called the "skirt." Soda jerks have been taught to provide a "neat, inviting skirt" around each dip.

The long Sundae spoon has been construed as a phallic symbol.

GOING THROUGH THE MOTIONS

Academy Award winning actress Loretta Young once revealed how she maintained a rapturous expression on her face during countless takes. She confessed that whenever she was in the arms of a dashing, leading man, she pretended she was face to face with a Hot Fudge Sundae.

Sex Therapist Pauline Falstrom asserts in *Sex is Like a Hot Fudge Sundae* that the Sundae and *amour* are comparable because "both are gooey and taste good. And, when taken slowly and with the right ingredients, both are fun."

If you gulp a Sundae down so rapidly that you hardly take time to enjoy it, appreciate its taste and feel, then you likely have a similar problem in bed, she suggests.

Falstrom recommends eating your Sundae very slowly. Taste the coldness of the vanilla ice cream, then notice how it feels in contrast to the hot fudge. Contemplate the iced goblet and the long-handled silver spoon. Savor the provocative placement of the ground walnuts on real whipped cream, explore their crunchy texture, then examine the contrast between the nuts and the softness of the cream. Save the plump red cherry for last.

Connections between Sundaes and sensuality are not new. Frederic Prokosch in *Voices: A Memoir* described an evening in Paris in 1922: "That night for dessert we had a Singapore Ice Cream, which was studded with ginger and covered with whipped cream. Gertrude Stein looked very voluptuous as she licked at her spoon, which she did with half-closed eyes and a slow, stately rhythm. Her tongue suggested the bow of an expert fiddler who is playing a languid and delicious adagio."

Redbook, a magazine directed at young mothers, recently commissioned a survey of women to find out what activity gave them the most pleasure. "Having sex with your husband or boyfriend" edged out "Eating a Hot Fudge Sundae"—but barely.

Cosmo girls faced more frankly sensual choices when queried by their favorite magazine. Those surveyed responded that "Playing hide

---

NOT
GOING THROUGH THE MOTIONS
❦

"*I'm at the age where food has taken the place of sex in my life. In fact, I've just had a mirror put over my kitchen table.*" – RODNEY DANGERFIELD

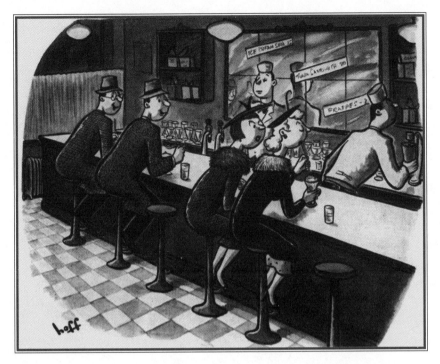

and seek with the cherry" was great sex play, but that "Licking whipped cream off each other's bodies" was even better. It's not a stretch to think that the perfect pastime for most women is having a Sundae *and* having sex. And, I dare say, for most men, too.

Samuel Butler wrote, the senses "are all a kind of eating. They are all touch, and eating is touch, carried to the bitter end."

And from Jean-Francois Revel: "To as great a degree as sexuality, food is inseparable from imagination."

Gael Greene has compared great food to great sex: "The more you have the more you want." In *Bite*, she rhapsodizes over Sundaes: "I sing of the do-it-yourself Sundae freakout with a discriminating hoard of haute toppings—wet walnuts, hot fudge, homemade peach conserve . . . inspiring a madness that lifts masks, shatters false dignity and bridges all generation gaps."

There was more going on than just a trip to the soda fountain as you listened to Jen in an episode of *Dawson's Creek*: "First you need to admire the Sundae, watch the Sundae. And just before it's about to drip, you gently let your lips lick around the exterior, savoring every inch. You want to make that Sundae last a long time. But not too long, cause otherwise it ends up all over the table instead of inside your mouth. But Dawson,

CHOCOLATE TO WEAR

Tom and Sally Fegley opened a small chocolate shop in the Vermont town of Brattleboro in 1989. When a friend they call "Dirty Larry" requested enough chocolate to make himself into a human Sundae, they obliged by packaging a cream-based ice cream topping in a jar labeled Chocolate Body Paint, with directions that read: "Heat to 98.6 degrees. Apply liberally, and let your imagination run free."

"Finger painting is the preferred method of application," says Sally. "But when we started selling to Henri Bendel, the department store's buyer insisted we include a small brush."

Might not a jar of chocolate on the nightstand start rumors?

"Perhaps," answers Sally, "but we sell over 100,000 jars of Chocolate Body Paint each year."

if you remember one thing, let it be this. If you don't get the whipped cream all over your face, you're not doing it right."

Stendahl remarked, upon tasting ice cream for the first time, "What a pity this isn't a sin!"

But Stendahl didn't live in the 21st century and he wasn't American. He instinctively understood, probably with every pore, the sensuality of ice cream, and he probably wouldn't have been surprised at how we spiritual descendants of the Puritans have excelled at wrapping sin, sex and Sundaes into luscious temptations.

Some adventurous New Yorkers remember the Saturday Night Sundae, a creation of the Erotic Bakery, which offered several frankly sensual desserts during the 1980s and '90s. The very description of how this was made was intended to titillate: Stack three canned pineapple rings on top of each other, and stand a banana upright in the center. Dip a scoop of ice cream on each side of the banana. Scoop out a small indentation at the end of the banana, spoon a dollop of whipped cream in the hollow . . . I think you get the idea.

Sophia Loren noted that sex appeal is fifty per cent what you've got and fifty per cent what people think you've got. A personal favorite in the sexy Sundae department was the Sophia Loren Sundae, devised by a pastry chef at the old New York Trattoria. This culinary embodiment of the Italian film goddess consisted of rum-soaked sponge cake topped with fruit syrup, and two large scoops of gelato placed side by side, each topped with a whole strawberry and a pignoli nut.

THIS 1950's PAINTING IS ALL INNOCENCE . . . UNLESS ONE PAUSES TO CONSIDER THE RESPEC-TIVE SHAPES OF THE ICE CREAMS AND THE YEARNINGS OF THE COUPLE.

DAYS OF WINE AND SUNDAES

*I*n "*Great Wines Made Simple*," *Andrea Immer* compares drinking a glass of wine to eating a *Hot Fudge Sundae*. She explains how the sensation in a spoonful of the cold and creamy vanilla combined with the hot and gooey fudge is similar to the mix of scents and tastes in just one sip of a complex wine. But which wine should you serve with a *Hot Fudge Sundae*? *Immer* recommends *Moet & Chandon Nectar Imperial*, which she calls "*equally indulgent*."

THE RECIPES

SINFUL CHOCOLATE SUNDAE

DIP 2 LARGE SCOOPS OF DOUBLE-CHOCOLATE ICE CREAM INTO A TALL SUNDAE GOBLET. COVER ONCE WITH MARSHMALLOW SYRUP, COVER AGAIN WITH HOT FUDGE SAUCE. INSERT 2 HEATH BARS INTO EITHER SIDE OF THE ICE CREAM, GARNISH WITH WHIPPED CREAM AND PLACE A HERSHEY'S KISS AT THE TOP.

– MAD MARTHA'S, VINEYARD HAVEN, MASSACHUSETTS

GUILTY CONSCIENCE

PLACE A 4-INCH BROWNIE SQUARE AT THE CENTER OF A PLATE. DIP 2 SCOOPS OF VANILLA ICE CREAM ON TOP OF THE BROWNIE. COVER WITH HOT FUDGE SAUCE, GARNISH WITH WHIPPED CREAM AND PLACE A MARASCHINO CHERRY ATOP EACH ICE CREAM MOUND.

– EDGAR'S IN PIONEER DRUG, ELK POINT, SOUTH DAKOTA

Chapter 29

BRAVE NEW SUNDAES

"Steaks, cream pies, hot fudge——those were thought to be unhealthy; precisely the opposite of what we now know to be true."

– Doctor speaking in the year 2173 in *Sleeper* by Woody Allen

The Green Mill started life as a soda fountain during Prohibition, but when it was granted St. Paul's first liquor license after Repeal, draught beer replaced ice cream sodas in the tall glass mugs. There are now three dozen Green Mill restaurants, most in Minnesota, offering just the right dose of genuine pubbiness. They rake in awards for their zesty pizzas, which come in three styles. But their Ice Cream Sundae comes in one style: inside-out!

Todd King, President of Green Mill Restaurants, knows an original idea when he sees one, and he spotted this one in 1995. "The Inside-Out Sundae was the brainstorm of a guy from our Duluth store," reveals King. "It wasn't embraced originally, and then it almost became sort of cultish."

King is a scrappy, competitive guy whose background includes running a Dairy Queen franchise. But the Inside-Out Sundae is definitely not a fast-food candidate. It requires cumbersome, time-consuming preparation.

After the initial prep of toppings on the *outside* of tulips, the Sundae glasses are held in a freezer awaiting customers' orders. It's a real shame, too, since the toppings that end up on the outside are so good. But, even more distressing, you might be one of the kitchen crew who makes the exacting reverse Sundaes. "We sometimes punish crybabies who show up late for work by putting them on the Sundae detail," admits King.

So, what's the proper technique for eating one? According to King, from the bottom up—scrape the outside of the tulip glass before you dig in.

GREEN MILL'S INSIDE-OUT SUNDAE IS BIG IN MINNESOTA.

Love it or hate it, the Inside-Out Sundae is the wildest Sundae to catch on for some time. Its sense of humor is so odd that customers appear giddy as they eat their way around it.

But in another way, we've actually been consuming "inside-outs" for a long time, thanks to premium ice creams that have come to market stuffed with candy, fudge and a host of other "toppings."

Kindred spirits Ben Cohen and Jerry Greenfield, who met in a seventh-grade gym class in Merrick, New York, are well-known pioneers in

A PREDICTION THAT HASN'T COME TRUE (YET)

🍒

"*He remained obstinately gloomy the whole afternoon; wouldn't talk to Lenina's friends (of whom they met dozens in the ice-cream soda bar between the wrestling bouts); and in spite of his misery absolutely refused to take the half-gramme Raspberry Sundae which she pressed upon him. 'I'd rather be myself,' he said. 'Myself and nasty. Not somebody else, however jolly.'*" – ALDOUS HUXLEY, BRAVE NEW WORLD

the super-premium ice cream movement. They reunited after college, and, in 1978, with a $12,000 investment, Ben and Jerry opened a home-made ice cream shop in a renovated gas station in Burlington, Vermont. They not only made rich ice creams with quirky names from the cream of local cows, they spent years modifying equipment and production techniques so they could get huge gobs of the stuff other people plunked onto the top of ice cream *into* their ice cream. Ben and Jerry's became so successful nationwide that it allowed its founders to retire to other good causes.

Frankly, I'm of two minds about the top brands of super-stuffed ice creams. Once your ice cream is crammed full of candy bars, cookie dough and trail mix, adding anything more than a spoon seems excessive.

Even though a quick lick of a good ice cream beats having no Sundae at all, rushing through these inside-outs can't possibly duplicate the experience of sitting down to a real Sundae—its visual excitement, its relaxing effect and, most important, its mélange of tastes that depends on each ingredient being at *its* right stage of ripeness, texture and temperature.

And what's the rush all about? Most ice cream isn't going into cones for sandy kids on the beach. Adults in America eat three times more ice cream than children do. My hunch is that the sophisticated urbanites and suburbanites who savor carefully prepared entrees are the ones who are skimping on their ice cream pleasures.

HERE'S TO YOUR HEALTH

*L*ouis Lanza, a fitness enthusiast and a torchbearer for healthy eating. presides over the Organic Sundae Bar at Josie's in Manhattan. Lanza's way is to start with 2 scoops of non-dairy low-fat soy "ice cream" (flavors include vanilla, chocolate, Neapolitan, chocolate peanut butter and mint marble fudge). The chef tops the frozen flavored soy with the customer's sauce choice (soy caramel, hot chocolate or maple soy) and whipped cream, almonds, walnuts, biscotti crumbs or sliced bananas.

Still, the future of classical Sundaes looks brighter now than it did when the American love affair with fast food was at its height.

In 1964, almost sixteen years after the inception of McDonald's, founder Ray Kroc spearheaded his company's search for a dessert. McDonald's version of strawberry shortcake flopped and was replaced by eat-in-your-hand fried apple pie. This was more successful but, understandably, demand for the pie never matched the enthusiasm for the chain's burgers and fries.

Finally, in 1978, McDonald's Corporation turned its attention to Sundaes. It's hardly a secret that McDonald's was the greatest single factor in subverting the longevity of the downtown soda fountain and diner; so when the company made Ice Cream Sundaes cheap and convenient again, it only seemed fair. But the Sundae has both blessed and burdened the fast-food empire. Even in an almost pre-fab mode, it's simply not a *fast* enough food to squeeze up profitability.

McDonald's assembly line pace falters at Sundaes. Servers seem to work the ice cream machines in slow motion, twirling cups to catch the soft ice cream as it oozes down the machine's stainless steel spout to form gently sloping spires. Then the servers drizzle the ice cream with hot fudge, caramel, or strawberry. Some even take another moment just to admire their creations. At most outlets there is no whipped cream or cherry—that would slow things down even more. But hey, here's a wee pour-your-own sack of institutional peanuts. This Sundae satisfies some, but it awakens in others a craving for the real thing.

Another speedway to the future for Sundaes arrived, courtesy of NASA. The gift shop at the Air and Space Museum of the Smithsonian does a booming business in selling foil packets of freeze-dried space-flight ice cream. Would anyone down on earth voluntarily eat food with the consistency of Styrofoam?

Let the record note that when a U.S. astronaut returned from a three and half month stint aboard Space Station *Mir*, NASA administrator Daniel Goldin's welcoming words were: "I'm saving a Hot Fudge Sundae for you," and he meant the real thing.

THE RECIPES

INSIDE-OUT SUNDAE

4 ounces hot fudge
4 ounces caramel
¼ cup honey-roasted peanuts

1 scoop vanilla ice cream
4 ounces strawberry topping

1. PAINT HOT FUDGE ON HALF OF THE EXTERIOR OF A TULIP GLASS AND CARAMEL ON THE OTHER HALF.
2. SPRINKLE CHOPPED PEANUTS ON THE HOT FUDGE AND CARAMEL.
3. FREEZE THE GLASS FOR UP TO AN HOUR.
4. SCOOP VANILLA ICE CREAM INTO PRE-COATED GLASS.
5. COVER ICE CREAM WITH STRAWBERRIES AND TOP WITH WHIPPED CREAM AND CHERRY.
6. TOP CONTENTS INSIDE THE GLASS WITH HOT FUDGE.
7. DRIZZLE MEDIUM-SIZE ROUND PLATE WITH HOT FUDGE AND PLACE SUNDAE IN THE CENTER OF PLATE.
8. SPRINKLE PLATE WITH CHOPPED PEANUTS.

– THE GREEN MILL, ST. PAUL, MINNESOTA

THE
PINK FLAMINGO

$\mathcal{T}$he Disney company insisted on something special from the McDonald's Corporation for its restaurant inside its Florida theme park. Mickey D's is a 280-seat eatery, shaped like a cheeseburger, which offers both Sundaes and Banana Splits.

••

DIP 2 LARGE SCOOPS OF STRAWBERRY ICE CREAM INTO A SUNDAE CON-TAINER, AND COVER WITH CRUSHED STRAWBERRIES. GARNISH WITH WHIPPED CREAM, SPRINKLE WITH RAINBOW JIMMIES, AND PLACE A CHERRY AT THE TOP.

••

– MICKEY D'S, WALT DISNEY WORLD, ORLANDO, FLORIDA

THE INVENTION THAT DID <u>NOT</u>
MAKE MILWAUKEE FAMOUS

$\mathcal{T}$he "Hot Scoop" microwave Sundae was the brainchild of the Wisconsin-based Johnston Company. Ice cream and syrup (fudge or butterscotch) were prepackaged in a cup designed to help keep the ice cream cool and the sauce warm. But some grocers did not put the product in the freezer as soon as it arrived. Consequently, the ice cream melted and became granular when it was finally refrozen. Unknowing consumers compounded the problem by dawdling on their way to their home refrigerators, thus setting up more freezer burn. Worse yet, not all microwave ovens are created equal; their heating power varies. After the cup was zapped, an unlucky Sundae lover might open it to find bumpy goo with lava-like syrup. Oops.

THE FINAL FRONTIER

The opening of Seattle's Space Needle Tower was timed to coincide with the opening of the 1962 Seattle World's Fair and its Century 21 theme. The rotating restaurant, five hundred feet above the city, offers a 360-degree view of Puget Sound, Lake Washington, Lake Union and the north end of downtown. The Space Needle Restaurant serves imaginative Pacific Northwest cuisine; its dessert specialty is the World Famous Lunar Orbiter. This Sundae is made with local Snoqualmie Gourmet Ice Cream, topped with a choice of berry coulis or chocolate fudge sauce, and garnished with freshly whipped cream. But what really makes it special is the presentation: The Sundae goblet, bedded on dry ice, is delivered to your table in a billow of rocket-to-the-moon clouds.

Open

Chapter 30

BACK TO THE FUTURE

"I believe the future is only the past again,
entered through another gate."

– ARTHUR WING PINERO

I believe that the Sundaes everyone will want tomorrow are the best Sundaes of yesterday. It's a matter not only of taste but also of values. While most of us find much to embrace in the cultural internationalism and communications speed of our time, we're all too keenly aware of the 21st century's unsettling qualities and real dangers. I don't need to chronicle for you all the reasons Americans crave unity, more tranquility and a return to reassuring traditions. You're here with me. We're both doing the best we can to lead our lives in the world as it is, looking backwards sometimes while also attempting to peer into the future.

That Sundae future in many locales is already here. It may be present in your community because it never went away. Or you may live near one of the many ice cream parlors, diners or other restaurants where kinder, gentler American cuisine is rooting itself. Influential restaurateurs across the country emulate Sundaes in desserts bearing other names, and that also points to a happy future of the Sundae in America.

But my bet is that Sundaes appear undisguised on more menus at this moment than they did when this century dawned.

In food-forward circles from coast to coast, today's catch phrase is "comfort food" a harking back to what many of us most love to eat. Coffee shops, diners and other all-American restaurants, places that almost invariably offer Sundaes, are reappearing in urbane neighborhoods. There are lines outside each E. J.'s Luncheonette in Manhattan for Sunday brunch.

Not long ago, Ira Freehof left the Waldorf Astoria to remodel a midtown coffee shop that he reopened as Comfort Diner. Then he repeated the trick on the Upper East Side. Freehof's restaurants, like similar

SUNDAES ARE OUR PAST AND FUTURE FOR A SIMPLE REASON: THEY MAKE US HAPPY.

ones—and some still on the drawing boards—in other cities and suburbs have a slightly upscale take on traditional foods. "The food is not like your mom's, it's like your grandmom's," Freehof, a New Englander, explains.

The assumption is that grandmother probably did more home cooking than her daughters did, and naturally used fresh ingredients. The three great comfort dishes, according to Freehof, are "macaroni and cheese, mashed potatoes and Ice Cream Sundaes."

No fuss is made over the three Sundaes a Comfort Diner offers, all prepared with house-made hot fudge sauce. The implication is that Sundaes, of course, belong on any authentic American menu. When everything else has you down, says Freeman, a Sundae "makes your soul feel better."

Sheldon Fireman is another New York restaurateur who believes in the future of the Sundae. The afternoon we spoke the former college linebacker, dressed in black T-shirt and rumpled sports jacket, boasted that he produces $40 million in annual sales from about 100 square yards of mid-town real estate. He stops to remind his audience that he grew up poor, in the Bronx. "I should be more humble," he admits. "I think, maybe some day they're gonna call me back."

As a youth, Shelly worked at Krum's ice cream parlor, across from Loew's Paradise movie theater, on the Grand Concourse. "We loaded the truck with ice cream according to the ethnicity of the neighborhood," he recalls. "If it was a Jewish section, the delivery was mostly chocolate; in the Irish sections, vanilla; the Italian neighborhood's favorite flavor was coffee. The job paid thirty-five cents an hour, and I wasn't allowed to accept tips."

At age 14, he was promoted to Saturday soda jerk. "Krum's was the largest confectionery in the Bronx, with maybe two hundred stools at the counter," he recalls. "They were famous for Ice Cream Sundaes, and I made more of them than I could ever count."

The cash registers at his six Manhattan restaurants tell him that New Yorkers like antipasti, dancing shrimp, sizzling steak—and hot fudge on their Sundaes. "There are only two questions to ask about food," maintains Fireman. "Is it good and is it authentic? People are open to new ideas, but not if it means disturbing their food history. Our customers want reassuring dishes—food designed less to impress than simply to enjoy."

When Shelly thinks about what to put on a menu, he addresses his hypothetical diner: "I want you to eat food you have an urge for, food that's in your memory bank." He says. "The Sundae stands the test of time, even in our famously fickle industry. Everyone loves the Ice Cream Sundae."

At Shelly's New York, in the same storefront that once housed a Horn & Hardart Automat, the most spectacular Sundae is called Mama's Mixing Bowl—a family-size wooden bowl of warm chocolate ganache (equal parts of melted chocolate and cream) and chocolate cookie crumbles, topped with chocolate ice cream, served with a wooden spoon filled with whipped cream, for mixing in.

It was Aldous Huxley who wrote, "The secret of genius is to carry the spirit of the child into old age." Great Sundaes, I believe, allow grown-ups to be children as they eat them, and kids to feel a natural part of a universe of treats, where age doesn't matter. Mama's Mixing Bowl is such a Sundae. But then so is a simple Hot Fudge Sundae.

Another of Fireman's restaurants, Brooklyn Diner USA, on West 57th Street, displays a mural of Ebbets Field, the Dodgers' stadium that was razed thirty years ago. New Yorkers and out-of-towners, the well-known (Sarah Jessica Parker and Monica Lewinsky, for example) and the unknown come here for dessert. There's little chat between tables here; diners are too intent on their ice cream and hot fudge. It's not about sex and the city; it's about Sundaes and the city, if the truth be known.

I could tell you that I've focused on New York for this chapter about the authentic future, because if Sundaes can still make it here, they can make it anywhere. And there'd be some honesty in that. But as we both now know, great Sundaes have many homes. And if there's not a good Sundae place near enough to you—well, I'm fairly certain your refrigerator has a freezer.

Seek and you shall find.

THE RECIPES

HOT FUDGE SUNDAE

LADLE 2 OUNCES OF HOT FUDGE SAUCE INTO THE BOTTOM OF A TALL SUNDAE GLASS. DIP ONE LARGE SCOOP OF VANILLA ICE CREAM INTO THE GLASS, AND ADD 3 OUNCES OF HOT FUDGE SAUCE. DIP ANOTHER 2 LARGE SCOOPS OF VANILLA ICE CREAM AND ADD ANOTHER 3 OUNCES OF HOT FUDGE SAUCE. DIP ONE MORE LARGE SCOOP OF VANILLA ICE CREAM AND COVER WITH A HEAPING TABLESPOON OF WET WALNUTS. GARNISH WITH WHIPPED CREAM, AND PLACE A STEMMED MARASCHINO CHERRY AT THE TOP.

–BROOKLYN DINER USA, NEW YORK, NEW YORK

Sundae Index

COURTESY OF BRAUM'S